Get Rich with Dividends

Get Rich with Dividends

A PROVEN SYSTEM FOR EARNING DOUBLE-DIGIT RETURNS

Second Edition

Marc Lichtenfeld

WILEY

Published by John Wiley & Sons, Inc., Hoboken, New Jersey.

The first edition of Get Rich with Dividends was published by John Wiley & Sons, Inc. in 2012.

Published simultaneously in Canada.

For general information on our other products and services or for technical support, please contact our Customer Care Department within the United States at (800) 762-2974, outside the United States at (317) 572-3993 or fax (317) 572-4002.

Wiley publishes in a variety of print and electronic formats and by print-on-demand. Some material included with standard print versions of this book may not be included in e-books or in print-on-demand. If this book refers to media such as a CD or DVD that is not included in the version you purchased, you may download this material at http://booksupport.wiley.com. For more information about Wiley products, visit www.wiley.com.

Library of Congress Cataloging-in-Publication Data:

Lichtenfeld, Marc.
    Get rich with dividends: a proven system for earning double-digit returns / Marc Lichtenfeld.—Second edition.
        pages cm
    ISBN: 978-1-118-99413-9 (cloth); ISBN: 978-1-118-99415-3 (ePDF);
    ISBN: 978-1-118-99414-6 (ePub)
        1. Dividends. 2. Portfolio management. I. Title.
        HG4028.D5L53 2015
    332.63′221—dc23   2014044967

Printed in the United States of America

20 19

For Holly, Julian, and Kira, who have made me rich
in the most important way

Contents

Foreword

When it comes to the stock market, most investors prefer glamour to profits.

Why do I say this? Tell average investors about a company with a cutting-edge technology, an exciting Phase III drug, or a new gold strike and they are all ears. But tell them about a blue chip stock with steady sales, a big order backlog, and a rising dividend yield and they are more likely to stifle a yawn.

That's unfortunate. Because, contrary to what most investors believe, startling innovation is not a good predictor of business success. Or, as the famous industrialist and steel magnate Andrew Carnegie succinctly put it, "Pioneering don't pay."

A young company that is just feeling its oats—and retaining all its earnings—is unlikely to be the best long-term investment. It's a widely recognized fact that 80% of new businesses fail in the first five years.

What really makes money for investors over time—and without the hair-raising volatility of hypergrowth stocks—is steady businesses paying regular dividends.

For example, over the past decade, with dividends reinvested, oil producer Chevron Corp has returned 200%. Altria Group, the U.S. tobacco giant, has returned more than 300%. Even musty old Con Edison, originally founded as New York Gas Light Company—a utility that was born 23 years before Thomas Edison—has returned 130% over the period.

In this excellent new book, my friend, colleague, and fellow analyst Marc Lichtenfeld shows you how and why to invest in great dividend stocks. And let me make two things clear at the outset. Number one, you could not find a more worthy, knowledgeable, or trustworthy guide to the investment landscape. And, second, this investment approach really works.

How can I be sure? Marc runs the Oxford Club's Perpetual Income Portfolio, a portfolio based solely on growth and income investments. He has done a superb job. In fact, when I looked at the returns recently, I had to ask him, "Holy crap, Marc. How do you do it?"

Fortunately, Marc shows you how you can earn returns like this yourself. He has made me a believer. At investment seminars today, I tell attendees, if you are looking for growth, invest in dividend stocks. If you are looking for income, invest in dividend stocks. If you are looking for safety, invest in dividend stocks.

Why? Earnings may be suspicious due to creative accounting. Revenues can be booked in one year or several years. Capital assets can be sold and the value listed as ordinary income. But cash paid into your account is a sure thing, a litmus test of a company's true earnings. It's tangible evidence of a firm's profitability.

Regular payouts impose fiscal discipline on a company. And history reveals that dividend-paying stocks are both less risky and more profitable than most stocks.

Dr. Jeremy Siegel, a professor of finance at the Wharton School of the University of Pennsylvania, has done a thorough historical investigation of the performance of various asset classes over the last 200 years, including all types of stocks, bonds, cash, and precious metals. His conclusion? High-dividend payers have outperformed the market by a wide margin over the long haul.

There is an awful lot of fear and anxiety about the economy andthe stock market today. Investors are understandably confused and uncertain about what to do with their money.

Marc Lichtenfeld has your solution. He demonstrates that even during market declines, dividend-paying stocks hold up better than non-dividend-paying stocks and often fight the broad trend and rise in value. The reason is obvious: These tend to be mature, profitable companies with stable outlooks, plenty of cash, and long-term staying power.

Bear in mind that U.S. companies are sitting on a record amount of cash right now, more than $2 trillion. Companies are not hiring, and they're not boosting spending. So a lot of this cash is rightfully going back to shareholders. The Dow currently yields more than bonds. And dividend growth among U.S. companies has averaged 10% per year over the last two years, more than double the long-term dividend growth rate.

The current outlook is especially promising. Over the last 50 years, for instance, the highest 20% yielding stocks in the

Standard & Poor's 500 returned 14.2% annually. That's good enough to double your money every five years—or quadruple it in ten. And if you were even more selective, say investing only in the ten highest-yielding stocks of the 100 largest companies in the S&P 500, your annual return would have been even better, 15.7%.

I should add the standard caveat here about past performance and point out that there are risks with dividend stocks too. As Marc points out, an investor would be foolish to plunk down money for a stock just because the dividend is large. You have to be selective. The market is full of "dividend traps," troubled companies that pay hefty dividends to keep investors from bailing out.

In the pages that follow, you'll learn how to avoid those and zero in on potential winners. Marc shows you how to look at cash flow and payout ratios and whether the dividend is sustainable.

Does this require a bit of legwork? Yes, but the payoff is large.

It astonishes me that investors are willing to lend money to the U.S. Treasury for the next ten years at less than 2%. What a terrible bet, one that virtually guarantees a negative, real (after inflation) return over the next decade.

A far better bet is a diversified portfolio of dividend-paying stocks. Over the eight decades through 2010, dividends contributed 44% of the U.S. stock market's return, according to Fidelity Investments. Sometimes it was much more. During the 1970s, for example, dividends generated 71% of returns.

Marc makes a strong case that dividend stocks today represent a historic opportunity. Not only are U.S. companies flush with cash, but payouts are less than one third of profits, a historic low.

Dividends alone won't generate a mouth-watering return. But they will rise over time—and surprising things happen when you reinvest them. Picture a snowball rolling down hill.

Albert Einstein understood this. As he observed, money compounding "is the most powerful force in the universe." And the best way to compound your money? Great companies that pay steady, rising dividends.

This book is your key because Marc Lichtenfeld does a great job of showing you just where to find them.

Alexander Green

Preface

It was a eureka moment.

I was working on a dividend spreadsheet, changing the variables, when the size of the numbers I saw surprised me. I realized that if my kids' money was invested according to the formula I was working with, they should never have any financial problems in adulthood, no matter what job or career they choose.

I also recognized that using the same formula, my wife and I should never have to worry about income in retirement.

And last, I understood that if my parents invested according to the formula, they, too, should have no worries about income in old age.

That's when I knew I had to write this book.

Get Rich with Dividends is for the average investor—the investor who is just getting started and the investor who is playing catch-up, the investor who has been burned by the booms and busts of the recent past and the investor who trusted the wrong advisor and ended up paying thousands of dollars for worthless advice.

This book is for all investors who are serious about creating real wealth for themselves and their families, investors who are willing to learn a simple system for making their money work as hard as they do (or did). It's easy to learn and implement and takes very little free time. Importantly, it's not a theory. It's been proved to work over decades of bull and bear markets.

And it's designed for investors who have other things they'd rather do than spend hours on their portfolios. Implement the 10–11–12 System and let stocks and time work their magic. All that's required is the occasional check-in from you to make sure the companies in your portfolio are still behaving the way you expect them to. If they are (and you'll learn how to pick companies that are most likely to meet your expectations), no further action is necessary.

As the editor of the Oxford Club's *Oxford Income Letter*, I receive e-mails every month from investors who are yearning for higher yield. In this low-rate environment, current yields aren't cutting it for many retirees. I was inspired to find a strategy that would ensure investors will not be in the same boat in the future as today's income seekers, who are taking on too much risk by chasing yield.

The 10–11–12 System outlined in *Get Rich with Dividends* will enable investors to achieve yields of at least 11% (and possibly much more) in the next 10 years—all while investing in some of the most conservative stocks in the market. These are companies with track records, some decades long, of taking care of shareholders. And if you don't need the income today, 12% average annual total returns (which crush the stock market average) are easily attainable. Earning 12% per year more than triples your money in 10 years, quintuples in 15 years, and grows by well over 10 times in 20 years. In other words, earning an average of 12% per year for 20 years turns a $100,000 portfolio into nearly $1.4 million. And that's with no additional investments.

What would an extra $1.4 million mean to you in retirement? First of all, it might spin off enough income that you wouldn't need to touch the principal. The money could be used for vacations with your family, a grandchild's college education, or peace of mind that you'll always have the best medical care.

Perhaps most important, you'll learn how my 10–11–12 System can still enable you to earn significant yields and double-digit returns in flat or down markets. Despite the nastiest bear market, you'll be sleeping comfortably, even smiling, once you implement my 10–11–12 System.

As you make your way through this book, you'll learn everything you need to know to become a successful investor. It's easy to read and even easier to get started.

In Chapters 1 and 2 we go over why dividend stocks are the best kind of investment you can make for the long-term health of your portfolio. Since you don't want to invest in just any old company paying a dividend, we discuss the special kind of stocks that you should select and how to find them.

I don't expect you to simply take my word for the claims I'm making, so in Chapter 3 I show you how I arrived at the various numbers, taking you through examples of how your income and total return can grow every quarter, with an example of how the 10–11–12 System still works and even thrives in bear markets.

In Chapter 4, we look at the big picture and the reason companies pay dividends. You'll understand why it's an important factor in determining the health of a business.

You'll see why certain conservative stocks are your best bet in Chapter 5. There's no reason to take excess risk to achieve your goals when some of the most conservative stocks on the market will achieve better results.

Chapter 6 discusses some interesting types of stocks you may not be aware of—stocks that typically yield more than regular dividend payers.

In Chapter 7, we lay the foundation for your portfolio, and then Chapter 8 is where you'll learn all about the 10–11–12 formula that you'll use to set you and your family up for long-term, double-digit yields and returns.

In Chapters 9, 10, and 11, we go over dividend reinvestment plans (DRIPs), foreign stocks, and options—all ways to turbocharge your returns.

Chapter 12 discusses everyone's favorite subject—taxes. Even if you use a CPA to do your taxes for you, be sure to read Chapter 12 as there is important information that could make your investments much more tax efficient.

And we wrap it all up in the conclusion and set you on your way to a lifetime of market-crushing returns and nights of worry-free (at least about your portfolio) sleep.

The strongest endorsement of the 10–11–12 System that I can make is this: I'm using it for my investments and for my kids' money as well.

Writing this book has been a labor of love because I know there will be thousands of families who will achieve financial freedom, be able to send a kid to college, make a down payment on a house, and enjoy retirement as a result of following the 10–11–12 System.

I'm glad yours will be one of them.

1

Why Dividend Stocks?

Let me start by making a bold statement: The ideas in this book are one of the most important gifts you can give to yourself or your children. On the pages that follow is the recipe for generating 11% yields and 12% average annual returns for your portfolio—significantly more if the stock market or your particular stocks cooperate.

I'm not trying to brag. I wasn't the one who first came up with the idea of investing in dividend growth stocks. I just repackaged it in a compelling, easy-to-read book that you will cherish for a lifetime and want to buy more copies of for all your friends and family, or at least lend them yours.

Enough jokes (for now). What I did was create an easy-to-learn system for investing in dividend growth stocks. You'll not only understand why dividend growth investing is one of the most lucrative and uncomplicated ways to invest but also learn the simple steps of how to do it.

If you follow the ideas in this book and teach them to your children, it's very conceivable that many of your concerns about income in the future will be over. And perhaps just as important, if your children learn this strategy at a young age, they may never have financial difficulties. They will have the tools to set themselves up for income and wealth far before they are ready to retire.

Keep in mind that I cannot teach you or your kids how to save money. If you would rather buy a new car at the expense of putting money away, I can't and won't attempt to fix that. This book is for the people who already know how to save and are trying to make that money work as hard as they do.

As far as saving money is concerned, the only advice I'll offer can be found in one of my favorite finance books, *The Richest Man in Babylon,* by George S. Clason. In that book, first published in 1926, Clason writes: "For every ten coins thou placest in thy purse take out for use but nine. Thy purse will start to fatten at once and its increasing weight will feel good in thy hand and bring satisfaction to thy soul."

Many personal finance gurus proclaim the same advice, but with a more modern bent to it, stating, "Pay yourself first."

Even if you are not able to save 10% of your current income, saving anything is crucial. As you will see, the money you save and invest using the ideas in this book will grow significantly over the years. So if you can save only 8% or 5% or even 2%, start doing it now. And if you get a raise or an inheritance or win the football pool, do not spend a dime of it until you have put away 10% of your total income.

Here's a scary statistic. According to a 2013 survey by the Employee Benefit Research Institute and Mathew Greenwald & Associates, 57% of American workers had less than $25,000 saved for retirement, with half of those people reporting less than $1,000 saved (see Table 1.1).[1]

Table 1.1   Total Savings and Investments Reported by Workers in 2013 (not including value of primary residence or defined benefit plans)

Amount Saved	Percentage of Workers
Less than $1,000	28%
$1,000 to $9,999	18%
$10,000 to $24,999	11%
$25,000 to $49,999	9%
$50,000 to $99,999	10%
$100,000 to $249,999	12%
$250,000 or more	12%

Source: Employee Benefit Research Institute and Mathew Greenwald & Associates, *2013 RCS Fact Sheet #3: Preparing for Retirement in America,* 2013, accessed November 15, 2014, www.ebri.org/files/Final-FS.RCS-13.FS_3.Saving.FINAL.pdf

And in 2013, the average 65-year-old's 401(k) account had just $25,000 in it.[2]

If you are serious about improving your family's financial future—and I know you are because you're investing the time to read this book—start saving today, if you haven't already.

Imagine if you saved 10% of your money and put it into the kinds of dividend stocks discussed in this book. Over time, your wealth should grow to the point that it will have generated significant amounts of income, perhaps even replacing the need to work.

This is the last point I will make about saving. You didn't spend your money on this book (or drive all the way to the library) just to have me beat you up about saving. Instead, I will assume you really are serious about securing your future and want to learn how to take those funds and add a few zeros to the end of the total number in your portfolio.

And if you're already retired and you need income right away, the strategies in this book can help you, too. You may not have the ability to compound your wealth, but you can invest in companies that will generate more and more income for you every year. Not only can you beat inflation, but you can also give yourself and even your loved ones an extra cushion.

There are lots of ways to invest your hard-earned money. But you'll soon see why investing in dividend stocks is a conservative way to generate significant amounts of wealth and income. This isn't theory. It's been proved over decades of market history.

Some people believe that real estate is the only way to riches. Others say the stock market is rigged so that the only people who make money are the professionals—therefore, you should be in the safety of bonds. Still others trust only precious metals. None of these beliefs is true at all.

Within the stock market, there are various strategies that are valid. Value investors insist you should buy stocks when they're cheap and sell when they're expensive. Growth investors believe you should own stocks whose earnings are growing at a rapid clip. Momentum investors suggest throwing valuation out the window and investing in stocks that are moving higher—and getting out when they stop climbing.

Still others trust only stock charts. They couldn't care less what a company's earnings, cash flow, or margins are. As long as it looks good on the chart, it's a buy.

Each of these methodologies works at some point. The effectiveness of value and growth strategies tend to alternate: One will be in favor while the other is out until they trade places. For one stretch of time, value stocks outperform. Then for another few years, growth will be stronger. Eventually, value will be back in fashion.

Whichever is in vogue at the moment, supporters of each will come up with all kinds of statistics that prove their method is the only way to go.

The same dynamic applies when it comes to fundamentals versus technicals. The technical analysts who read stock charts assert that everything you need to know about a company is reflected in its price and revealed in the charts. Fundamental analysts, who study the company's financial statements, maintain that technical analysis is akin to throwing chicken bones and reading tea leaves.

There are plenty of other methodologies as well. These include quantitative investing, cycle analysis, and growth at a reasonable price (GARP), to name just a few more.

Die-hard supporters of all these strategies claim that their way is the only way to make money in the markets. It's almost like a religion whose most fanatical followers act as if their beliefs are the only truth—period, no debate, end of story. They're right and you're wrong if you don't believe the same thing they do.

I'm no authority when it comes to theology. But when it comes to investing I know this: Dogma does not work.

You will not consistently make money investing only in value stocks. Again, sometimes they're out of favor. If you only read stock charts, sometimes you'll be wrong. Charts are not crystal balls. Quantitative investing tends to work until it doesn't. Just ask the investors in Long-Term Capital Management, which lost everything in 1998.

Long-Term Capital was a $4.7 billion hedge fund that utilized complex mathematical models to construct trades. It made a lot of money for investors for several years. It was supposed to be fail-safe. But like the *Titanic,* which was also supposed to be unsinkable, Long-Term Capital hit an iceberg in the form of the Russian financial crisis and nearly all was lost.

"Y'all Must've Forgot"

During his prime, legendary boxer Roy Jones Jr. was one of the best fighters that many fans had ever seen. However, Jones didn't seem to get as much respect as he thought he deserved. So, in 2001, he released a rap song that listed his accomplishments and reminded fans about just how good he was. The song was titled "Y'all Must've Forgot." Roy was a much better fighter than he was a rapper. The song was horrendous.

Looking back, investors in the mid to late 1990s remind me of boxing fans in 2001, when Roy released his epic tribute to himself. Both groups seemed to have forgotten how good they had it—boxing fans no longer appreciated the immense skills of Jones, and investors grew tired and impatient with the 10.9% average annual returns of the Standard & Poor's (S&P) 500 (including dividends) since 1961. After decades of investing sensibly, in companies that were good businesses that often returned money to shareholders in the form of dividends, many investors became speculators, swept up in the dot-com mania.

I'm not blaming anyone or wagging my finger. I was right there with them. During the high-flying dot-com days, I was trading in and out of Internet stocks, too. My first "10 bagger" (a stock that goes up 10 times the original investment) was Polycom (Nasdaq: PLCM). I bought it at $4 and sold some at $50 (I sold up and down along the way).

However, like many dot-com speculators, I got caught holding the bag once or twice as well. I probably still have my Quokka stock certificate somewhere in my files. Never heard of Quokka? Exactly. The company went bankrupt in 2002.

With stocks going up 10, 20, 30 points or more a day, it was hard not to get swept up in hysteria.

And who wanted to think about stocks that paid 4% dividends when you could make 4% in about five minutes in shares of Oracle (Nasdaq: ORCL) or Ariba (Nasdaq: ARBA)?

Did it really make sense to invest in Johnson & Johnson (New York Stock Exchange [NYSE]: JNJ) at that time rather than eToys? After all, eToys was going to be the next "category killer," according to BancBoston Robertson Stephens in 1999. It's interesting to note that eToys was out of business 18 months later and BancBoston Robertson Stephens went under about a year after that.

If, in late 1998, you'd invested in Johnson & Johnson, a boring stock with a dividend yield of about 1.7% at that time, and reinvested the dividends, in mid 2014, you'd have made about 8.6% per year on your money. A $3,000 investment would have nearly quadrupled.

Johnson & Johnson is a real business, with real products and revenue. It is not as exciting as eToys or Pets.com or any of the hot business-to-business (B2B) dot-coms that took the market by storm.

But 16 years later, are there any investors who would complain about an 8.6% annual return per year? I doubt there are very many—especially when you consider that the S&P 500s annual return, including reinvested dividends, was just 4.2% during the same period.

Now, you might have gotten lucky and bought eBay (Nasdaq: EBAY) at $2 per share and made 16 times your money. Or maybe you bought Oracle and made five times your money. But for every eBay and Oracle that became big successful businesses, there were several Webvans that failed and whose stocks went to zero.

In the late 1990s, the stock market became a casino where many investors lost a ton of money and didn't even get a free ticket for the buffet. It doesn't seem that we've ever completely returned to the old way of looking at things.

My grandfather, a certified public accountant who owned a seat on the New York Stock Exchange, didn't invest in the market looking to make a quick buck. He put money away for the long term, expecting the investment to generate a greater return than he would have been able to achieve elsewhere (and possibly some income).

He was willing to take risk, but not to the point where he was speculating on companies with such ludicrous business ideas that the only way to make money would be to find someone more foolish than he to buy his shares. This is an actual—and badly flawed theory used by some. Not surprisingly, it is called the Greater Fool Theory.

There were all kinds of companies, TheGlobe.com, Netcentives, and Quokka, to name just a few, whose CEOs declared we were in a new era: This time was different. When I asked them about revenue, they told me it was all about "eyeballs." When I pressed them about profits, they told me I "didn't understand the new paradigm."

Maybe I didn't (and still don't). But I know that a business has to eventually have revenue and profits. At least a successful one does.

I'm 100% certain that if Grandpa had been an active investor in those days, he wouldn't have gone anywhere near TheGlobe.com.

One principle that I believe many investors have forgotten is that they are investing in a business. Whether that business is a retail store, a steel company, or a semiconductor equipment manufacturer, these are businesses run by managers, with employees, customers and

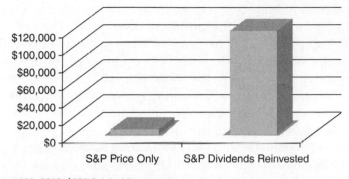
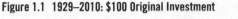

Figure 1.1 1929–2010: $100 Original Investment
Source: Chart: Marc Lichtenfeld; data: Ned Davis Research

equipment, and, one hopes, profits. They're not just three- or four-letter ticker symbols that you enter into Yahoo! Finance once in a while to check on the stock price.

And these real businesses can create a significant amount of wealth for shareholders, particularly if the dividend is reinvested.

According to Ed Clissold of Ned Davis Research, if you'd invested $100 in the S&P 500 at the end of 1929, it would've grown to $4,989 in 2010 based on the price appreciation alone. However, if you'd reinvested the dividends, your $100 would've grown to $117,774. Clissold says that 95.8% of the return came from dividends.[3] (See Figure 1.1.)

Marc Lichtenfeld's Authentic Italian Trattoria

Years ago, my wife and I were in Ashland, Oregon. We loved the town and started talking about escaping the rat race, moving to Ashland, and opening a pizza place. We've repeated that conversation on trips to Banff in the Canadian Rockies; Asheville, North Carolina; and even Tel Aviv, Israel.

Considering that I know nothing about the restaurant business, would not be happy if not in close vicinity to a major American city, and am a lousy cook, the pizza joint remained a happy fantasy.

But for the purposes of this book, Marc Lichtenfeld's Authentic Italian Trattoria will serve as an example of a business with revenue and profits. We're also going to assume that I'm your brother-in-law (your sister was always a very good judge of character) and you've agreed to become my partner in the business.

One day I come to you, my favorite brother-/sister-in-law, with my plans for the restaurant. I have the space lined up. It's in a popular location with a lot of foot traffic. I've been talking with a wonderful young chef who is eager to make an impression on local diners and critics. All that's missing is start-up capital.

This is where you come in. In exchange for a $100,000 investment, you will receive a 10% ownership stake. I show you my projections: The restaurant will break even the first year and make $100,000 in the second year and $200,000 in the third year.

One of the questions you may have is how will you get your money back. Do you have to wait for the restaurant to be sold, or will you receive some of the profit each year?

If I tell you that my goal is to build the business to $1.5 million in sales and then sell it for two times sales ($3 million), where you'll receive $300,000, your response might be very different from what it would be if I tell you that half the profits will be invested back in the business with the other half split up among the partners in a yearly payout (dividend).

Your decision on whether to give me the money will depend in part on your goals. Are you willing to speculate that you'll receive the big payoff in several years when the business is sold, or would you rather receive an income stream from your investment but no exit strategy (plan to sell the restaurant)?

When buying stocks, investors have to make similar decisions. Do they buy a stock with the sole purpose of selling it higher down the road, or do they buy one that provides an income stream and opportunities for income growth in addition to capital gains?

I don't know about you, but if I'm investing in someone's business, I want to see some money as soon as possible rather than wait for an exit strategy.

Here is another factor that might affect your decision to invest in my trattoria: Instead of offering to pay you your cut of the profits every year, I might offer to reinvest that money back into the restaurant and give you more equity. That way, your piece of the profits gets larger each year. Eventually, you can start collecting a significant cash payout annually, or receive a bigger slice of the pie when you sell your stake in the business because your equity has increased above your original 10%.

This last scenario is the same as reinvesting dividends, a method that is the surest way I know of to create wealth.

And what I love about this strategy is that it works (and has worked) no matter who is President of the United States; what happens in Europe, Iran, or the Middle East; how high unemployment and inflation are; and so on. Sure, those things will affect your short-term results, but over the long haul, they mean nothing and in fact could help you accumulate more wealth, as I'll explain in the section on bear markets in Chapter 3.

The Numbers

Investing in dividend stocks is the best way to make money in the stock market over the long term.

But don't just take my word for it. Harvey Rubin and Carlos Spaht II, both of Louisiana State University in Shreveport, write, "For those investors who adopt ten and fifteen year time horizons, the dividend investment strategy will lead to financial independence for life. Regardless of the direction of the market, a constant and growing dividend is a never-ending income stream."[4]

Just a few pages ago, I told you that dogma doesn't work, yet here I am sounding fairly dogmatic. The proof that dividend investing creates wealth is in the numbers.

First of all, investing in the stock market works. Since 1937, if you invested in the broad market index, you made money in 69 out of 76 rolling 10-year periods, for a 91% win rate. That includes reinvesting dividends.

The seven 10-year periods that were losers ended in 1937, 1938, 1939, 1940, 1946, 2008, and 2009. The periods 1937 to 1940 and 1946 were tied to the Great Depression. The 10-year periods ending 1936 to 1940 were brutal with an average decline of 40%. The decade ending in 1946 was much tamer with a loss of 11%. The 2008 and 2009 10-year periods each lost 9%.

Paul Asquith and David W. Mullins Jr. of Harvard University concluded that stocks that initiated a dividend and increased their dividends produced excess returns for shareholders. Additionally, the larger the first dividend payment and subsequent dividend raises, the larger the outperformance.[5]

And research shows that dividend stocks significantly outperform during market downturns.

Kathleen P. Fuller and Michael A. Goldstein of Babson College concluded, "Dividend-paying stocks outperform non-dividend-paying stocks by 1 to 2% more per month in declining markets than in advancing markets."[6]

In recessions, the outperformance is even more pronounced. During the recessions of 2001 and 2008, the Dividend Aristocrat index (more on Aristocrats in the next chapter) outperformed the S&P 500 by 6.45 percentage points annually, according to Albert Williams and Mitchell Miller of Nova Southeastern University.[7]

Later on in the book, I'll show you how you can achieve double-digit yields, which would nullify the effects of even the weakest historical markets performance and enable you to make money regardless of what the overall market is doing.

Think back to other methods that I mentioned at the beginning of the chapter: value, growth, and technical analysis. They all work—sometimes. No system, strategy, or methodology that I know of has a 91% win rate that can approach 100% when the dividends have been reinvested for a while.

Oh, I know, but it's different this time. We're in an unprecedented period of debt, unemployment, financial crises, and everything else unpleasant under the sun.

Things were pretty lousy in 2009, with the entire financial system on the precipice of collapse. Nevertheless, the market came roaring back, doubling in two years and tripling in five.

Similarly, there was little to get excited about during the 1970s—with mortgages and inflation in the teens and each U.S. President less popular than the last. Yet the 10-year return on the market was positive every year throughout the 1970s and 1980s (encompassing years from the 1970s).

Since 1937, the average cumulative rolling 10-year total return on the stock market is 128%. This includes the seven negative 10-year periods. Since 1999 (the first year the 10-year data was available), the S&P Dividend Aristocrat index's 10-year rolling return average has been 183% and was positive every year, with the lowest 10-year return of 40% in the period ending in 2008 (when the market tanked 38% that year), compared with a 9% loss for the S&P 500 in the 10 years ending in 2008 (and a loss of 26% when you exclude dividends).

I recently read a government official's estimate (and we know how accurate government officials usually are) that, over the next 10 years, stocks will lose 13% because of baby boomers taking their money out of the market.

I don't think that's likely. As I've shown you, historically, there's a 91% chance of the market giving you a positive return over 10 years. Additionally, where are the baby boomers going to put their money? Bonds are paying ridiculously low interest rates right now. Is it worth it to lock up your funds for 10 years to earn 2.5%? That won't even keep up with inflation.

For that little, I'd rather invest in a stock with a 4% or 5% yield and take the risk that in 10 years, the stock will at least be where I bought it today.

But you know what? Even if the stock falls, you can still make money.

Let's assume you buy 500 shares of stock at $20 for a total of $10,000. It pays a dividend of $1 per year or a yield of 5%. Now, this company has a long history of raising its dividend every year. Over the next 10 years, it raises the dividend by an average of 5% per year.

Let's also assume that the government official was right and the stock tracks the market and falls 13%.

If you reinvest your dividends for the next 10 years, while the dividend is increasing and the stock price is falling, you'll wind up with about $17,000. That's a 70% increase, or a compounded annual growth rate of 5.45%—despite a *decline* in stock price of 13%!

But what if you invested in a 10-year treasury, paying 2.5% per year? After 10 years, you would get your $10,000 back, plus collect $2,500 in interest for a total of $12,500, or a compound annual growth rate of 2.26%.

So in this example, your stock investment lost 13% in price yet still more than doubled the performance of a 10-year bond where your principal is guaranteed.

Think about that for a moment. Your stock lost value, but because you reinvested your dividends, you more than doubled your return on the guaranteed principal of the 10-year bond. And that takes into account a drop in the market over a 10-year period that would be equal to the fifth largest in the last 76 years.

Oh, and if you decide after 10 years to start collecting the dividend instead of reinvesting it, then you'd receive $1.63 per share, up from $1 per share. And because you reinvested the dividends, you're collecting that $1.63 per share on 1,000 shares instead of your original 500. So your yield is going to be over 16% on your original investment. This alone should convince you to run out and buy dividend stocks. As they say on TV, but wait, there's more.

Keeping Up with Inflation

People don't talk much about inflation these days. Since 1914, the average inflation rate in the United States is 3.4%. But inflation has been extremely low since the Great Recession in 2008. That was the last time we saw inflation above the historical average. In fact, from 2009 to 2013, the average annual inflation rate was a miniscule 1.6%.

Inflation of 3.4% seems pretty tame, especially for any of us who remember the 1970s and 1980s when inflation hit double digits. But even at 3.4%, your buying power is cut in half after 20 years.

Because inflation is low today, people underestimate its erosive powers. Despite the fact that for the past decade inflation has averaged a point and a quarter below the historical 3.4% figure, buying power has still been cut.

What would have cost $1,000 in 2004 cost $1,259 in 2014.

And what if you're saving for something whose price rises faster than the average 3.4% rate, such as college tuition or retirement (and the associated medical costs)?

For example, in 2011, the College Board reported that tuition at public four-year universities increased 8.5%. The following year, the cost rose 4.5%.

Where are you going to find an investment that will grow 8.5%? Today, if you lock up your money for 20 years in a treasury, you'll be lucky to get 3% per year.

Let's see how cost increases could affect tuition fees in the future. Right now, tuition for in-state students at a public university averages $8,893. Private university students are paying an average of $30,094. Over the past decade, college tuition has increased 79.5%. Should this trend continue, in 18 years you'll have to shell out $35,241 per year for the public university and $119,258 for the private school. And that doesn't include room and board (or beer). Sure hope your kid can hit a jump shot.

So, if you're lucky enough to be able to buy $100,000 worth of Treasuries for your newborn child's education, and they pay 3% per year, you should be close to where you need to be to pay tuition for four years. But you'll still have to come up with some cash for room and board, books, and more (beer). But remember, this is just an in-state school. At the private university, forget it. You need to average more than a 9% compound return per year to hit your target.

This is an extreme example, but you can see that Treasuries are a tough way to fund any future expense. One of the problems with fixed income is that you can't reinvest it to let it compound the way you can with dividend stocks.

As you'll soon see, a 12% compounded annual return is readily achievable when you invest in stocks that pay dividends. In fact, if you reinvest those dividends, there is no reason why you shouldn't be earning 12% per year, over the long run.

12%. That was not a typo. You can earn that much per year (and even more) by investing in boring, large-cap, dividend-paying companies that simply match the overall return of the market. And at 12% per year, all you need to do is start off that college fund with $1,000 and add $2,000 per year, and the in-state school is entirely paid for by the time your little boy or girl graduates high school.

We're not taking any extra risk here. We're not investing in speculative companies with new technologies that may or may not work. All we are doing is trying to match the market with companies that have a long track record of paying shareholders. But through the system I'm about to show you, it can help you achieve your financial goals.

You need to know which types of dividend stocks to buy in order to achieve the maximum returns. So now, let me show you.

The 10–11–12 System

When starting the process of writing *Get Rich with Dividends,* my objective, besides spreading the gospel of dividend investing, was to give readers a process for achieving their financial goals. The method had to have three simple but key components.

1. It had to be easy to understand and implement.
2. It had to work.
3. It had to be inexpensive.

I've read truckloads of financial books and products in my lifetime, many claiming to have an easy system that would make me rich. The problem was they usually didn't work. Often they weren't easy to use, nor were they cheap.

For example, one book I read recommended buying tax lien certificates and explained how I could make 16% per year on those investments.

Maybe somebody has achieved those kinds of results, but when I checked with offices of various county governments around the country that were selling those certificates, I found I'd be lucky to make a few percentage points on my money. And the process was far from easy or inexpensive.

Other strategies have recommended changing my entire portfolio every year, incurring hundreds of dollars in commission charges, even with a cheap discount broker.

So I set out to create a system for investors that would be so easy to use and so inexpensive, they'd be free to devote their energies to things that really excite them, like their families, friends, work, and hobbies, rather than having to spend countless hours working on and constantly adjusting their portfolios.

If you're the kind of person who likes to check stock quotes during the day, research companies, and follow business news—that's great. You and I will have a lot to talk about if we meet.

But most people want to invest and more or less forget about it, checking in only occasionally to make sure everything is going according to plan.

The result is the 10–11–12 System. It is designed so that, in 10 years, the investor will be generating 11% yields and will have averaged a 12% *annual* return on his or her portfolio. Just to be clear, you won't achieve a total return of 12% in year 1. But by year 10, your average annual return over the entire 10-year period should be 12%.

It is so easy to use that my then-10-year-old son instantly grasped the concept and was excited about its prospects for his money when I explained it to him. He took his birthday and allowance money and bought shares in the kind of stocks I talk about in the book, understanding his funds should more than double by the time he gets to college.

And other than the commission on buying the stocks when you set up the portfolio, it doesn't have to cost you *anything* after that.

Simple, easy to use, and it works.

For example, Southern Company (NYSE: SO), which has raised its dividend every year for the last 10 years, returned 149% over the past 10 years when dividends were reinvested. This is a real-life example, not theoretical. After 10 years, a $10,000 investment in Southern Company was worth $24,892 versus the S&P 500, which would have been worth $22,718.

So, let's get started so that you can begin earning 12% returns right away.

Summary

- Save money—try to save 10% of your income to put to work in dividend-paying stocks. If you can't save 10%, start smaller and work your way up.
- Investing in dividend-paying stocks is the best way to create wealth in the stock market.
- Dividend stocks will help you beat the ravages of inflation, unlike Treasuries.
- The 10–11–12 System is designed to generate 12% annual returns over the long term, cost next to nothing, be extremely easy to implement, and take up very little of your time over the many years you'll use it.
- Roy Jones Jr. made one of the worst songs in the history of recorded music.

Notes

1. Employee Benefit Research Institute and Mathew Greenwald & Associates, *2013 RCS Fact Sheet #3: Preparing for Retirement in America,* 2013, www.ebri.org/files/Final-FS.RCS-13.FS_3.Saving.FINAL.pdf.
2. Edward Siedle, "The Greatest Retirement Crisis in American History," Forbes.com, March 20, 2013, www.forbes.com/sites/edwardsiedle/2013/03/20/the-greatest-retirement-crisis-in-american-history/.
3. Harvey Rubin and Carlos Spaht II, "Financial Independence Through Dollar Cost Averaging and Dividend Reinvestments," *Journal of Applied Business and Economics* 12, no. 4 (2011): 12.
4. Ibid.
5. Paul Asquith and David W. Mullins Jr., "The Impact of Initiating Dividend Payments on Shareholders' Wealth," *Journal of Business* 56, no. 1 (1983): 77.
6. Kathleen P. Fuller and Michael A. Goldstein, "Do Dividends Matter More in Declining Markets?" *Journal of Corporate Finance* 17, no. 3 (June 2011): 457.
7. Albert Williams and Mitchell Miller, "Do Stocks with Dividends Outperform the Market during Recessions?" *Journal of Accounting and Finance* 13, no. 1 (2013): 58, http://m.www.na-businesspress.com/JAF/MillerM_Web13_1_.pdf.

CHAPTER 2

What Is a Perpetual Dividend Raiser?

When I first got into the financial industry, I was an assistant on a trading desk, eventually working my way up to trader.

Before I knew how to analyze a company by reading balance sheets and income statements, I learned about stock charts.

Two key concepts in reading stock charts are:

1. The trend is your friend.
2. A trend in motion stays in motion.

Essentially, what these two concepts mean is that a stock will continue moving in the same direction until it doesn't anymore. How's that for insight?

But when you look at a chart of a stock that is heading higher, although there are some minor corrections, it often moves on a diagonal line (called a trend line) upward. Stocks traveling along one of these trend lines usually continue until something changes their direction. The cause of the change of direction could be a bad earnings report, bad economic data, or a large institution selling its shares. Frequently, once the trend is broken, the stock will reverse.

I bring this up because the same can be said about companies that raise their dividends.

Typically, a company with an established trend of increasing its dividends will raise them again next year and the year after that and the year after that . . . unless it becomes impossible to do so. Management knows that investors have come to expect the dividend increase every year and any change in that policy will send them running for the exits.

I call these companies Perpetual Dividend Raisers, and they come in more than one variety.

Dividend Aristocrats

The concept of a Dividend Aristocrat is simple. A Dividend Aristocrat is a company that is a member of the Standard and Poor's (S&P) 500 index and has raised its dividend every year for at least 25 years.

These are primarily blue chip companies with long histories of growing earnings and dividends.

If your investing goals are to impress your friends at cocktail parties with your knowledge of brand-new technology and to brag about the millions of dollars you will make off of the companies behind those technologies—well, then, Dividend Aristocrats aren't for you.

Most people don't find a company like Genuine Parts (NYSE: GPC), which makes auto replacement parts, to be terribly exciting. I'm not even sure Genuine Parts' CEO is all that excited about replacement parts.

But the company makes a ton of money—$685 million in 2013— and it has increased its dividend every year since 1956. That is pretty exciting.

Think about that for a minute. Every year. Since 1956.

Through the Cuban Missile Crisis, the Kennedy assassinations, Vietnam, Watergate, gas lines, the Cold War, the rise of Japan, the rise of China, 9/11, the dot-com collapse, the housing bust, the Red Sox winning the World Series, and the Great Recession—through all of these difficult, and in some cases tragic, events, when pundits were saying the sky was falling, at times when the economy really did stink and was even on the verge of collapse, like in 2008, Genuine Parts went about its business, making and selling auto parts and returning more money to shareholders than it did the year before.

The last time Genuine Parts did *not* increase its dividend, President Eisenhower was in the White House, and Elvis Presley made his television debut on *The Louisiana Hayride* on KSLA-TV in Shreveport, Louisiana.

That was a long time ago.

And that is pretty darn exciting.

The Index

The Dividend Aristocrat index is currently made up of 54 companies and is rebalanced every year. If a company raises its dividend for the twenty-fifth consecutive year, it is added to the index the following January. If a company fails to raise its dividend, it is removed.

To qualify to be an S&P Dividend Aristocrat, a stock must meet these four criteria:

1. Be a member of the S&P 500 index.
2. Have increased its dividend every year for at least 25 years in a row.
3. Have a market capitalization of at least $3 billion on the day the index is rebalanced.
4. Trade a daily average of at least $5 million worth of stock for the six months before the rebalancing date.

In 2013, four companies—AbbVie (NYSE: ABBV); Chevron Corp. (NYSE: CVX); Cardinal Health, Inc. (NYSE: CAH); and Pentair (NYSE: PNT) were added to the index, while one company, Pitney Bowes (NYSE: PBI), was dropped. There were no changes in 2014.

Each company is given equal weight in the index. This means that the size of the company isn't a factor in the calculation of the performance of the index. A company with a $20 billion market cap has the same impact on the index as a $40 billion company.

Some other variables can affect a company's ability to be placed in the index, such as sector diversification. But these other considerations don't come into play often. The most important factors are 25 years of consecutive dividend increases and being a member of the S&P 500.

The index is great for showing you all kinds of performance statistics as to why Dividend Aristocrats make excellent investments and how they outperform the S&P 500. But you can't buy the index. Surprisingly, as of this writing, there is only one exchange-traded fund (ETF) that tracks the S&P 500 Dividend Aristocrat index. The ProShares S&P 500 Aristocrats ETF (Nasdaq: NOBL) launched in October 2013.

An ETF is a fund that is bought and sold like a stock. It often tracks an index or sector and is passively managed—meaning an investment manager is not actively making buying and selling decisions based on the economy, market, or a company's prospects. Stocks in an ETF are bought and sold based on their inclusion or weighting in an index or sector.

There is, also, an ETF that is based on the S&P High Yield Dividend Aristocrats index. This index is made up of the 60 highest-yielding members of the S&P Composite 1500 that have raised their dividends for 25 years in a row.

This ETF is called the SPDR S&P Dividend ETF (NYSE: SDY). It attempts to track the performance of the S&P High Yield Dividend Aristocrats index.

And although it might be tempting to buy the either of the ETFs for convenience purposes, I *do not* recommend buying or owning it for several reasons.

- *It's too new.* The ProShares S&P 500 Aristocrats ETF is less than a year old as I write this. There is not enough performance or dividend data to know whether this fund will replicate the performance of the index or whether the dividend will consistently climb. In fact, the ETF's third quarterly dividend in June 2014 was 8% lower than the previous quarter.
- *You have no control over the sector weightings.* For example, 22% of the High Yield ETF's portfolio is invested in the financial industry. That is not particularly surprising, as financials are often among the highest-yielding stocks. But you should have more control over your own portfolio and invest according to the way you see fit.
- *The High Yield ETF lacks a long track record.* The SPDR Dividend ETF has been around only since 2007. Aristocrats have at least a 25-year track record. Achievers, which we discuss later, have at least a 10-year track record. The purpose of investing, according to the ideas laid out in this book, is to put your money in stocks with a long history of rewarding shareholders by increasing the dividend. As it turns out, the SPDR Dividend ETF *lowered* its dividend in 2009.

- *In many cases, we can find higher yields in individual stocks rather than these ETFs.*

There are no mutual funds dedicated to Dividend Aristocrats at this time.

The Champions

Dividend Aristocrats represent the bluest of the blue chips—big, solid companies with two-and-a-half-decade or longer track records of raising dividends.

However, with roughly 50 stocks qualifying to be included in the index in a given year, we need to expand our universe—especially because not every Aristocrat has a decent yield. Just because a company has raised its dividend for 25 years in a row doesn't mean it has an attractive dividend yield.

The yield could have started very small and grown at a minuscule pace. Or the stock could have gotten hot, running up in price and decreasing the yield. For example, Aristocrat Sherwin-Williams (NYSE: SHW) has raised its dividend for 36 consecutive years but still yields only 1.1%.

Therefore, we need to look in other places for companies with juicy yields that have a history of growing the dividend.

Enter the Champions.

The DRiP Resource Center (http://dripinvesting.org) maintains a list called the Dividend Champions. These stocks are similar to the Aristocrats in that the companies have raised their dividends for at least 25 consecutive years. However, they are not required to be part of the S&P 500 and have no liquidity or other restrictions. Just the 25-year track record with an annual dividend boost. That's the only qualification.

I love the name Champions because it reminds me of my favorite sport, boxing, and that a person doesn't need to be six feet three and 240 to be a successful professional athlete.

I've seen grown men who weigh 125 pounds walk into an arena and be given the same respect (or even more) by an adoring crowd as if they were the heavyweight champion of the world.

Some of the small stocks on the Champions list also prove you don't have to be big to be successful. More than a few have market caps of under $1 billion yet are still terrific income investments.

For example, Tompkins Financial Corp. (NYSE: TMP) is a Dividend Champion. Tompkins, a small bank based in Ithaca, New York, has a market cap of just $665 million and trades an average of 30,000 shares per day. Compare that with an Aristocrat, such Kimberly Clark (NYSE: KMB), which has a market cap of $40 billion and trades 1.3 million shares a day.

As we look at Table 2.1, the list of Champions includes—but is not limited to—Dividend Aristocrats. Typically, the Champions list has more than twice the number of stocks as the Aristocrats.

Dividend Aristocrats are always Dividend Champions because they've raised their dividend for 25 years in a row—but a Dividend Champion might not be a Dividend Aristocrat if the stock is not in the S&P 500.

Some of the stocks on the Champions list offer benefits to individual investors that may not be attainable by professional money managers. Some Champions are rather small, so an institutional investor, such as a mutual fund manager, would not be able to buy stock without moving the price considerably. Additionally, the manager might have a tough time selling the stock because of liquidity issues.

For example, if a mutual fund manager wanted to own a few million shares of California Water Service Group (NYSE: CWT), it would be tough to either accumulate or sell stock when the time comes, considering that it trades fewer than 140,000 shares per day.

Table 2.1   Perpetual Dividend Raisers

Name	List Maintained By	Requirements	Notes
Dividend Aristocrats	Standard & Poor's	Annual dividend raised 25 years in a row Member of S&P 500 Liquidity requirements	Included on Champions list
Dividend Champions	DRiP Resource Center	Annual dividend raised 25 years in a row	Includes Aristocrats
Dividend Achievers	Nasdaq OMX	Annual dividend raised 10–24 years in a row Liquidity requirements	Included on Contenders list
Dividend Contenders	DRiP Resource Center	Annual dividend raised 10–24 years in a row	Includes Achievers
Dividend Challengers	DRIP Resource Center	Annual dividend raised 5–9 years in a row	

Source: Standard & Poor's, Nasdaq OMX, and DRiP Resource Center

However, an individual investor who wants to pick up several thousand shares or fewer would have no problem buying or selling them in the marketplace. In this case, the individual investor has more flexibility than the money manager with millions at his or her disposal.

The professional money manager can invest only in stocks that are large enough to handle the influx of money and must buy enough shares to make a difference to the fund's performance. The individual investor can buy or sell without affecting the stock or attracting much notice. The ability to purchase stocks that are inaccessible to professionals is one way individual shareholders can outperform institutional money managers.

As you conduct your research on Perpetual Dividend Raisers, you'll find plenty of stocks that don't trade much volume but are great little companies with long histories of dividend increases that you'll be able to buy but the fund manager at Fidelity and Vanguard will have to pass up.

Junior Aristocrats

At any given time, there are usually only about 50 Dividend Aristocrats and roughly 100 Champions. The exact totals at this moment are 54 Aristocrats and 107 Champions.

Although 107 stocks sounds like a lot, keep in mind that, like the Aristocrats, not all of them have attractive yields. Despite annual raises, many still have yields below 3%. So we need to expand our choices even further.

The next groups of stocks are the Dividend Achievers and Contenders.

Dividend Achievers are stocks that have raised their dividends for 10 or more consecutive years and meet very easy liquidity requirements.

Moody's Investor Services started the list in 1979, and it is now maintained by Nasdaq OMX.

Interestingly, although there is only one ETF that tracks the Dividend Aristocrats, several follow Dividend Achievers.

The Vanguard Dividend Appreciation ETF (NYSE: VIG) tracks the Nasdaq US Dividend Achievers Select index.

The Powershares Dividend Achievers (NYSE: PFM) tracks the Broad Dividend Achievers Index. An important difference between the Dividend Achievers Index and the Broad Dividend Achievers Index is that the Broad Index can include real estate investment trusts (REITs) and master limited partnerships (MLPs). Those stocks often have higher yields. We discuss REITs and MLPs in Chapter 6.

The PowerShares High Yield Equity Dividend Achievers Portfolio (NYSE: PEY) corresponds to the Nasdaq US Dividend Achievers 50 Index. The Achievers 50 Index consists of the top 50 highest-yielding stocks that have raised their dividends for at least 10 straight years. These stocks also must trade a minimum of $500,000 worth of stock per day in November and December before the index is reconstituted.

Just as Achievers are like junior Aristocrats, Dividend Contenders are like junior Champions.

The Aristocrats and Achievers lists are maintained by two institutional financial firms: S&P and Nasdaq. Both lists are reconstituted once per year. The Champions and Contenders lists are maintained and dutifully updated every month by David Fish of the DRiP Resource Center.

The only thing a company has to do to qualify to be a Contender is raise its dividend every year for 10 to 24 years. Similar to the Champions, there are no liquidity or index requirements.

And just as all Aristocrats are Champions but not all Champions are Aristocrats, all Achievers are Contenders but not all Contenders are Achievers.

Champions and Contenders have the same time requirements as far as number of years of consecutive dividend raises as Aristocrats and Achievers, but the Champions and Contenders have no other restrictions.

Beneath the Contenders are Challengers. These are companies that have raised their dividends between five and nine years in a row. Challengers are also part of the compilation tracked by David Fish and the DRiP Resource Center.

You might automatically think that you should stick with Champions because of their long-term track record. After all, with a 25-year (or longer) history of boosting the dividend, the company is probably more likely to continue to raise the dividend than one with just a five-year record.

Typically, fewer than 10% of Champions fail to raise the dividend in any given year, while roughly 15% of Contenders and Challengers do not boost the dividend.

However, it's important to understand that because Champions are either more mature or have more mature dividend programs, their yields and dividend growth rates are often (but not always) lower than those of Contenders.

For example, as of August 2014, the average yield for a Champion was 2.64% versus 2.76% for a Contender and 3.00% for a Challenger. The most recent average dividend increases were 8.15%, 8.22%, and 12.69%, respectively. The current growth rates of Champions are higher than their 10-year average, but Contenders' and Challengers' most recent dividend hikes are lower than their average 10-year growth rates.

The difference seems small but gets magnified as the years go on. (See Table 2.2.)

As you can see from Table 2.2, if you invest in the average Champion, and each year the dividend grew by the same amount as in 2014, after 10 years your dividend yield would be 5.3%. In the case of the Contender, your yield would increase to 5.8%. If your original investment were $10,000, based on the given assumptions, in 10 years you'd collect $4,942 in income with the Contender and $4,728 from the Champion.

The Challengers, with their much higher dividend growth rates, blow away their more mature peers. After 10 years, the dividend yield surges to 8.6%, and the investor would have collected $5,372 in income.

As with most investments on Wall Street, the seemingly safer investment typically offers a lower yield and growth prospects—in this particular situation, I'm talking about dividend growth, but often share price growth is less for safer companies than those with more risk.

Table 2.2   Champions, Contenders, and Challengers

	Average Yield	Average Most Recent Dividend Increase	Yield in 10 Years*	Income Received over 10 Years ($10K invested)*
Champions	2.64%	8.02%	5.3%	$4,728
Contenders	2.76%	8.64%	5.8%	$4,942
Challengers	3.00%	12.42%	8.6%	$5,372

*Estimated
Source: DRiP Resource Center and Marc Lichtenfeld

Investors have to weigh their need for safety against their need for income or growth. A Dividend Contender or Achiever can still be a relatively safe stock. A company like Atmos Energy (NYSE: ATO), a Dallas-based natural gas distribution and transportation company, has boosted its dividend every year for 26 years. Since 1989, the stock has risen at a compound annual growth rate of 10.8% (not including dividends).

In the Challenger category, a company such as Columbia Sportswear (Nasdaq: COLM) has raised its dividend every year for nine years. During that time, the stock has risen 77%, or a compound annual growth rate of 6.6% per year.

Challengers, being earlier into their dividend-raising histories, tend to lift their dividends at a faster pace than Champions and Contenders. (See Table 2.3.)

Survivorship

From the statistics just cited, you might automatically think that investing in the Challengers is the better way to go. After all, they offer a higher yield and higher dividend growth rate. Besides, for the most recent dividend increases, their 1-, 3-, 5-, and 10-year dividend growth rates are higher as well.

However, you need to take into account survivorship—the fact that the companies we are examining are the ones that did not get dropped from the list of Challengers. In other words, there are some companies that you may have invested in years ago, expecting a never-ending increase in the dividend, that were cut because they failed to raise the dividend.

For example, up until February 2009, financial services firm F.N.B. Corp. (NYSE: FNB) had a 35-year history of raising its dividend. In the 10 years prior, the company grew its dividend by an average of 7.8% per year.

Table 2.3   Annual Dividend Growth Rates as of August 2014

	1 Year	3 Year	5 Year	10 Year
Champions	8.4%	7.5%	6.6%	7.9%
Contenders	9.8%	10.0%	8.9%	11.7%
Challengers	14.6%	18.6%	16.2%	19.0%

Source: DRiP Resource Center

However, in August 2008, after 35 straight years of dividend boosts, the company kept its $0.24 quarterly dividend the same as it was in the previous year and in February 2009 cut the dividend in half, where it remains today.

So F.N.B is no longer calculated in any growth rate or total return figures pertaining to Dividend Champions.

Gold miner Randgold Resources Limited (Nasdaq: GOLD) is a more recent example. From 2008 to 2013, the company raised its dividend from $0.10 per year to $0.50, an impressive compound annual growth rate of 30.8%. But in 2014, the company did not raise the dividend. Instead, Randgold kept the annual dividend at $0.50, disqualifying it from the Challengers list.

Later in the book, I show you that the odds are in your favor that your company will continue to raise the dividend every year—especially after you learn what to look for in a stock to ensure the safety of the dividend.

Summary

- Dividend Aristocrats are members of the S&P 500 that have raised their dividends every year for at least 25 years.
- Dividend Champions are any stocks that have raised their dividends for 25 consecutive years.
- Junior Aristocrats include companies that have raised their dividends between five and 25 years in a row.
- You're better off buying individual stocks rather than dividend ETFs or funds.
- Genuine Parts' CEO falls asleep at his desk because his business is so boring. (Okay, he probably doesn't. But no one would blame him if he did.)

CHAPTER 3

Past Performance Is No Guarantee of Future Results, but It's Pretty Darn Close

No doubt you've seen loads of advertisements for mutual funds that tell you how much money their funds made but then warn you that past performance is no guarantee of future results. Just because a fund is up 10% one year doesn't mean the managers will be able to repeat the feat the next.

In fact, quite often, top-performing mutual funds will underperform their benchmarks and their peers in the future.[1] According to a study by Baird, 85% of the top quartile of mutual fund managers underperformed their benchmark by one percentage point or more over any three-year period. And 50% underperformed by three percentage points.

A benchmark is a measure of performance against which a fund or portfolio is measured. The benchmark can be a broad market index, like the S&P 500, or it can be a narrower index, like the Nasdaq Biotechnology Index.

It would not be fair to measure a mutual fund that specializes in biotech against the S&P 500 since biotech stocks tend to be more volatile. For example, if the S&P 500 was up 10% for the year and the Nasdaq Biotech Index was down 5%, but a biotech mutual fund was up 5%—although it didn't perform as well as the overall market, it was much stronger than the biotech sector in general. That would likely be considered a successful year for the fund since it outperformed its benchmark.

But that's not necessarily the case when it comes to Perpetual Dividend Raisers. Although the future rise or fall of the stock price may correlate to how it's done in the past, the dividend should be very closely related.

Chances are, a company that has raised its dividend for 25 years in a row is going to do it again in year 26. And again in year 27. And in year 28. . . .

As I explain in the next chapter, there are very solid reasons that managements pay and increase dividends to shareholders. To change the company's dividend program (i.e., not raising the dividend) after several decades represents a dramatic shift in policy that is not taken lightly.

In 2014, no companies fell off the Dividend Aristocrat Index. All 54 companies continued to raise their dividends.

The prior year, 2013, one company was removed from the list— Pitney Bowes (NYSE: PBI)—but not because it failed to raise its dividend. It actually boosted the dividend slightly in 2012. The problem was its market cap fell below the $3 billion minimum.

Since then, the company's market cap has risen back above $3 billion, but the troubled company cut its dividend in half in May of 2013.

In 2012, only one company fell off the list. Between 2008 and 2012, the average number of companies deleted from the index each year was five. And remember, 2008 and 2009 were the years of the Great Recession. Not including those two very difficult years, we usually see only two or three stocks fall off the list—far less than 10% of the companies in the index.

So, in normal years, you have better than a 90% chance of seeing your Aristocrat company continue to raise dividends. And in years of financial collapse, roughly 80% of the companies continued to increase their dividends.

When you invest in Perpetual Dividend Raisers, you're banking on the ever-increasing income that they spin off or the tremendous wealth-building opportunity that compounding the reinvested dividend provides.

Chances are, you don't want to have to read earnings reports every quarter, wondering what the company's prospects are and whether it's generating enough cash to boost the dividend this year.

With Perpetual Dividend Raisers, you usually don't have to. The companies have proved after 15, 30, or even 50 years that they can deliver what their shareholders want, year after year, decade after decade.

That's what makes Perpetual Dividend Raisers so appealing. They are as hassle-free as you'll find in the stock market.

Now, that doesn't mean you should ignore your stocks. The portfolio we'll design in this book is meant for at least a 10-year holding period. You should still check in with each company from time to time and make sure the dividend is being paid, the dividend is raised annually, and no crisis is jeopardizing the dividend or the company's long-term health and prospects.

Even a solid, well-run company can occasionally step on a land mine, which changes its prospects and makes the reason you invested in it no longer valid.

However, if you can learn not to get affected by every little hiccup in the company's business, the way analysts freak out over often-insignificant line items, you'll be able to hang on to your stocks more easily, allowing time and compounding dividends to work for you.

If a company's executives are managing a business for the long-term benefit of its owners (shareholders), it really doesn't matter if they miss earnings estimates by a few cents per share in any given quarter. In fact, if the market overreacts, that's positive for investors who are reinvesting dividends because they'll be able to do so at lower prices.

Certainly be mindful of your stocks' businesses and long-term prospects, but don't make buy-or-sell decisions based on any one data point or piece of news.

As I show you in Chapter 5, one of the attractive features of investing in these kinds of stocks is how easy it is and how little time you need to devote to maintaining your portfolio. Don't get caught up in CNBC's hysterics or any other financial media's scary headlines that are designed to frighten you into hanging on their every word. And that's coming from someone who regularly appears on CNBC.

If you stay the course, for the most part, over the next 10 years, the portfolio you create of Perpetual Dividend Raisers will create an ever-increasing stream of income or build wealth—with very little work required from you.

Performance of Perpetual Dividend Raisers

It was never my thinking that made the big money for me. It was always my sitting.

—Jesse Livermore, legendary investor

Numerous studies show that companies that raise dividends have stocks that outperform those that don't.

According to Ned Davis Research, companies that raised or initiated dividends from 1972 to 2010 did significantly better than those that didn't. And the companies that did not pay a dividend or, heaven forbid, cut their dividend, weren't even in the same ballpark as the dividend payers and raisers.

After 38 years, the dividend cutters were worth only $82 after a $100 original investment, a compound annual growth rate of –0.52%. The nonpayers were worth a whopping total of $194, for a minuscule 1.76% annual return. Companies that paid a dividend but kept it flat were worth $1,610, or 7.59% annually. But the dividend raisers and initiators generated a compound annual growth rate of 9.84% and were worth $3,545. (See Figure 3.1.)

There's nothing wrong with 9.84% annually over 38 years. But a little later on, I show you how to generate at least 12% annual returns, which would turn that $100 into nearly $7,500 in the same period.

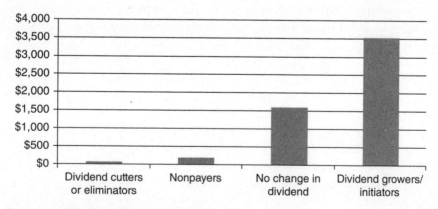

Figure 3.1   1972–2010: $100 Original Investment
Source: Ned Davis Research

Historically, the S&P Dividend Aristocrats index has outperformed the S&P 500. Since inception in 1990, Aristocrats have returned 901% versus the S&P 500, which returned 469%.

Interestingly, the only period the Aristocrats underperformed the overall market was during the late 1990s, when the dot-com bubble inflated nearly everything. Stable, so-called boring dividend stocks were out of favor as investors rushed into anything that had risk.

It was a "new paradigm," many experts said. "This time is different," they declared. You'd be throwing your money away investing in traditional blue chip companies. How could you invest in Coca-Cola (NYSE: KO) when you have the opportunity to invest in a white-hot growth stock, like Pets.com?

You can see from Figure 3.2, as soon as the market reversed and investors recovered their sanity, Aristocrats significantly outperformed the S&P from thereon after.

Additionally, Dividend Aristocrats outperformed the S&P 500 with less risk. Over the past 10 years, the index's standard deviation—a measure of volatility—was 13.6% versus the S&P 500s 14.7%, indicating that the Aristocrats are less volatile (risky) than the general market.

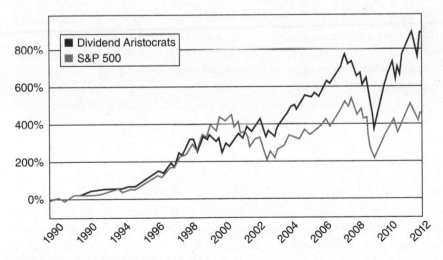

Figure 3.2 Dividend Aristocrats vs. S&P 500

Source: Standard & Poor's

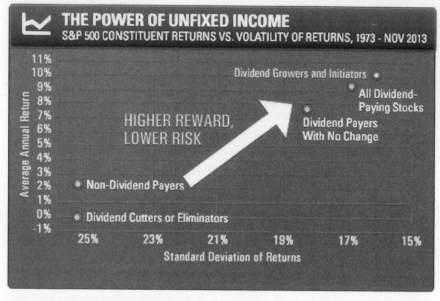

THE POWER OF UNFIXED INCOME
S&P 500 CONSTITUENT RETURNS VS. VOLATILITY OF RETURNS, 1973 - NOV 2013

Dividend Growers and Initiators

All Dividend-Paying Stocks

HIGHER REWARD, LOWER RISK

Dividend Payers With No Change

Non-Dividend Payers

Dividend Cutters or Eliminators

Average Annual Return

11% 10% 9% 8% 7% 6% 5% 4% 3% 2% 1% 0% -1%

25%   23%   21%   19%   17%   15%

Standard Deviation of Returns

Figure 3.3 The Power of Unfixed Income

Source: Chart: Alan Gula, *Dividends and Income Daily*; Data: Ned Davis Research

And you can see in Figure 3.3, which was created by Alan Gula at *Dividends and Income Daily*, that for the past 40 years, stocks that cut or didn't pay dividends had a lower rate of return, while investors had to endure greater risk as measured by standard deviation. Dividend growers and initiators (declaring dividends for the first time) had the highest return and lowest risk.

Another way to measure performance is the Sharpe ratio. Without getting into the complicated math, the Sharpe ratio measures how much return you are getting for the amount of risk you are taking.

It's a way of comparing investment returns when risk is considered. The higher the number, the better the risk-adjusted return.

The S&P Dividend Aristocrats index also outperformed the S&P 500 when it came to the Sharpe ratio, meaning that the Aristocrats outperformed the market not only on an annualized basis (11.8% versus 7.0% over 10 years) but also on a risk-adjusted basis. And the Aristocrats did so with less risk, as measured by the standard deviation.

Measuring Risk

There are various ways of measuring an investment's reward versus risk, including standard deviation and the Sharpe ratio. Standard deviation represents how much the stock's price will fluctuate within a 95% probability.

The Sharpe ratio is a numeric representation of how much reward an investor received versus the risk that was taken. The higher the number, the better.

It makes sense that investors who buy a biotech penny stock should expect a huge return on investment if it works out because they are taking on a large amount of risk. You wouldn't invest in a biotech penny stock to achieve 8% returns per year. You could achieve that by owning much less risky blue chip stocks.

Table 3.1 compares the risk and reward versus risk of the S&P Dividend Aristocrats index and the S&P 500.

As you can see from Figure 3.4, both the returns and the Sharpe ratio were higher for Dividend Aristocrats than for the S&P 500. This is important because not only are you making more money, but on a risk-adjusted basis, you are also outperforming the market.

Based on the data, you could say that over 10 years, Aristocrats returned three times as much as the S&P 500, when risk is taken into account.

It makes sense when you think about it. The extra dividend yield lifts total return and attracts income-oriented investors, which can increase demand for the stock. Additionally, the decades-long track record of raising dividends represents stability.

So not only are you taking less risk, but you're also making more money. Usually in the market it's the other way around. Riskier investments tend to have bigger payoffs (and more of a chance of a loss).

Let's look at an example of one Aristocrat.

Table 3.1   Aristocrats: Outperformance with Lower Risk, 2001–2011

	S&P Dividend Aristocrats Index	S&P 500 Index
Annualized total return	7.1%	2.9%
Standard deviation	18.4%	21.3%
Sharpe ratio	0.12	0.04

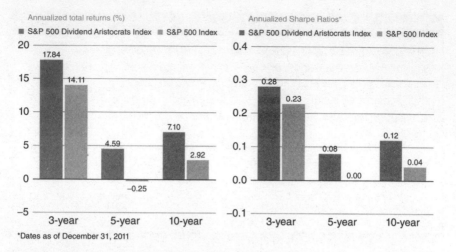

Figure 3.4 **Better Returns, Both Absolute and Risk-Adjusted**

Source: Legg Mason, *Carpe Dividends,* www.leggmason.com/individualinvestors/documents/ sales_idea/D9741-CarpeDividends InvestmentIdea_EIB_CBAX013016_public.pdf and Standard & Poor's

Chevron (NYSE: CVX) has raised its dividend every year for the past 27 years. Over the past 10 years, the dividend growth rate has averaged nearly 11% per year.

Including dividends, Chevron outperformed the S&P 500 154.9% versus 78.6% over the past decade. And while the yield on the stock as I write this is just 3.4%, the yield on the price you would have paid 10 years ago is 8.6%. (See Figure 3.5.)

So, if you had bought shares of Chevron 10 years ago, not only would your stock have doubled the return of the S&P 500, but you'd

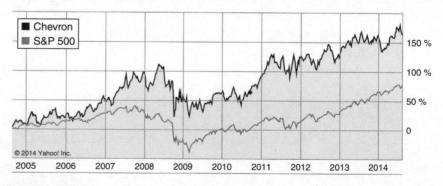

Figure 3.5 **Chevron**

Source: Yahoo! Finance

also be earning 8.6% on your money—a yield that today is associated with the junkiest of junk bonds rather than a blue chip company that has raised its dividend every year since The Bangles topped the charts with "Walk Like an Egyptian."

What if you had started on this program of buying Perpetual Dividend Raisers years ago?

Although the Dividend Aristocrats index officially started only in 1990, if you'd bought shares of Procter & Gamble (NYSE: PG) in 1981, *after* it had increased its dividend for the twenty-fifth consecutive year, your shares would have outperformed the S&P 500 by 1.7 percentage points per year: 11.3% versus 9.6%.

Your yield would now be 102% on your original investment. That's not a typo. In 1981, Procter & Gamble shares were trading for about $2.51 per share, adjusted for splits. Today, those shares pay an annual dividend of $2.57.

So each year, you'd be getting a dividend that surpasses what you paid for your shares.

Here are some unbelievable numbers.

If, in 1981, if you'd bought $10,000 worth of Procter & Gamble, at the end of 2013, your investment would be worth $337,821, and you would have collected $108,940 in dividend checks. If you'd reinvested the dividend, you would be looking at a nest egg of about $811,840 and own over 9,700 shares, now generating $25,093 per year in dividends, all from a $10,000 investment. Your annual yield would now be two and a half times your original cost.

In 1981, I was entering high school. I shoveled snow in the winter and did other odd jobs to make money. I was a great saver, even back then. If I had taken my savings from many birthdays and long winter days with my snow shovel, purchased $1,000 worth of Procter & Gamble, and never touched it, today it would be worth $81,000. That would be a nice chunk of change for anyone to buy a car, pay down a mortgage, put toward the children's college educations, or just have extra funds to relieve some financial pressure.

Do you know a teenager who might thank you every time he or she thinks of you in 30 years because of a $1,000 investment today?

Let's look at another example.

Johnson & Johnson (NYSE: JNJ) pays a dividend of $1.68 per share, or a yield of 2.7%. Not bad by today's standards, but nothing too exciting.

The company has raised its dividend every year for 52 straight years—right around the time Mick Jagger and Keith Richards formed a little blues band called the Rolling Stones. It was also the year of the Cuban Missile Crisis. In 1987, after the company had established its 25-year track record, if you had bought 100 shares, you'd have paid $3,900.

In the middle of 2014, it would be worth over $219,000, and you would have collected $57,524 in dividends. If you'd reinvested those dividends, your total would be worth over $401,000, and you'd have more than 1,100 shares spinning off over $6,504 a year in income, or a 43% yield on your original cost.

That compares to the S&P 500, which would be worth $49,580 for a similar investment.

Interestingly, Johnson & Johnson and Procter & Gamble's returns were almost identical—14.3% annually when dividends were reinvested. So how did a P&G investor end up with $410,00 more than an investor in J&J?

Simple. Procter & Gamble's figures were calculated from 1981. Johnson & Johnson's were from 1987. As you'll soon see in several examples, the longer you hold a stock and reinvest the dividends, the more the numbers jump.

Compounding takes a while to get started, but once it does, it's like a runaway train going downhill, picking up momentum each year. The longer you can hold on to a stock, the greater the returns should be.

These are two examples of Perpetual Dividend Raisers that grow their dividends at roughly 10% or more per year. Many have lower growth rates but have nevertheless increased their dividends every year for 30, 40, or 50 years.

The key to obtaining the incredible results shown in the two examples is to find companies that not only have track records of growing dividends every year but also raise dividends at a large enough rate so that they keep ahead of inflation and become wealth builders.

Why It Works

> Do you know the only thing that gives me pleasure? To see my dividends coming in.
>
> —John D. Rockefeller

To understand why Perpetual Dividend Raisers are able to generate such enormous returns over time, it is necessary to understand the concept of compounding.

Let's say you own 1,000 shares of a $10 stock that pays a $0.40 per share dividend, or a yield of 4%. In the first year, you will collect dividends of $400.

If the following year the company raises its dividend by 10%, you will collect $0.44 per share, or $440. In year 3, the company again boosts the dividend by 10%, so you receive $0.484 per share, or $484. Year 4 sees another 10% hike, so that year's dividend totals $0.5324, or $532.40. And so on.

Compounding is all about momentum. The first several years, it seems like not much is going on, but watch what happens once you get a few more years out.

Table 3.2 shows what your dividend, income, and yield would be each year if you owned the stock for 20 years and the dividend grew 10% per year.

You can see that it takes a little while for the dividend to grow significantly. In year 5, the yield has grown only 47%. But each year

Table 3.2   Watch What Happens if You Give Compounding Time

Year	Dividend per Share	Yearly Income	Yield on Original Investment
1	$0.40	$400	4%
2	$0.44	$440	4.4%
3	$0.484	$484	4.8%
4	$0.5324	$532	5.3%
5	$0.5856	$586	5.9%
6	$0.6442	$644	6.4%
7	$0.7086	$709	7.1%
8	$0.7795	$780	7.8%
9	$0.8574	$857	8.6%
10	$0.9432	$943	9.4%
11	$1.0375	$1,038	10.5%
12	$1.1412	$1,141	11.4%
13	$1.2554	$1,255	12.6%
14	$1.3809	$1,381	13.8%
15	$1.5190	$1,519	15.2%
16	$1.6709	$1,671	16.7%
17	$1.8380	$1,838	18.4%
18	$2.0218	$2,022	20.2%
19	$2.2240	$2,224	22.2%
20	$2.4464	$2,446	24.4%

that growth increases more and more. Year 6 has a dividend that is 61% higher than year 1's. Year 7 is 77% higher, year 8 is 95% higher, and by year 9, the dividend has more than doubled to 115% of the original. And it continues to grow at a rising pace.

After 10 years, you've collected $6,375 in income, or 64% of your original investment. After 20 years, you've amassed $22,910 in income, more than double your original investment.

Let's make a crazy assumption for a minute. Let's assume the stock goes absolutely nowhere during the entire time you own it. It remains completely flat.

Nevertheless, you'd generate income of $22,910, or a total return of 129%—during a completely flat market. Annualized, that comes out to 6.4% per year.

Now, if you reinvest the dividends, something truly amazing happens.

Again, assuming the stock remains perfectly flat during the entire time, after 10 years you would have 1,881 shares for an 88% total return, instead of a 64% return if you'd collected the dividends. After 20 years, your investment would be worth $94,880, a total return of 849%, a compound annual growth rate of 11.91%—in a stock whose price didn't budge.

Let's take a look at how this occurred. Table 3.3 shows 20 years' worth of quarterly dividends reinvested with no movement in stock price.

Notice how it takes 43 quarters to double the number of shares owned but only 13 more quarters to triple and 8 more quarters to quadruple. After that, ownership goes up by 1,000 shares at least once a year.

The power of compounding kicks into overdrive as the years go by.

But you have to be patient. In our example, in the first few quarters, the value is increasing only about $100 per quarter. The value of the portfolio doesn't increase by $1,000 until the ninth quarter—nearly two and a half years.

The next $1,000 level is reached in seven quarters, after four years and three months. Then again in six quarters. And then four. See a pattern?

After 10 years, the portfolio is increasing by about $500 per quarter. Four years later, the portfolio is rising by $1,000 per quarter.

Table 3.3   20 Years of Reinvesting Quarterly Dividends

Quarter	Quarterly Dividend per Share	# of Shares Owned	Total Quarterly Dividend	Stock Price	Value
Y1 Q1	$0.10	1,010	$100	$10	$10,100
Y1 Q2	$0.10	1,020.1	$101	$10	$10,201
Y1 Q3	$0.10	1,030.301	$102.01	$10	$10,303
Y1 Q4	$0.10	1,040.604	$103.03	$10	$10,406
Y2 Q1	$0.11	1,052.051	$114.47	$10	$10,521
Y2 Q2	$0.11	1,063.623	$115.73	$10	$10,636
Y2 Q3	$0.11	1,075.323	$117	$10	$10,753
Y2 Q4	$0.11	1,087.152	$118.29	$10	$10,872
Y3 Q1	$0.121	1,100.306	$131.55	$10	$11,003
Y3 Q2	$0.121	1,113.62	$133.14	$10	$11,136
Y3 Q3	$0.121	1,127.095	$134.75	$10	$11,271
Y3 Q4	$0.121	1,140.733	$136.38	$10	$11,407
Y4 Q1	$0.1331	1,155.916	$151.83	$10	$11,559
Y4 Q2	$0.1331	1,171.301	$153.85	$10	$11,713
Y4 Q3	$0.1331	1,186.891	$155.90	$10	$11,869
Y4 Q4	$0.1331	1,202.688	$157.98	$10	$12,027
Y5 Q1	$0.14641	1,220.297	$176.09	$10	$12,203
Y5 Q2	$0.14641	1,238.163	$178.66	$10	$12,382
Y5 Q3	$0.14641	1,256.291	$181.28	$10	$12,563
Y5 Q4	$0.14641	1,274.685	$183.93	$10	$12,747
Y6 Q1	$0.161051	1,295.214	$205.29	$10	$12,952
Y6 Q2	$0.161051	1,316.073	$208.60	$10	$13,160
Y6 Q3	$0.161051	1,337.269	$211.95	$10	$13,373
Y6 Q4	$0.161051	1,358.805	$215.37	$10	$13,588
Y7 Q1	$0.177156	1,382.878	$240.72	$10	$13,829
Y7 Q2	$0.177156	1,407.376	$244.99	$10	$14,073
Y7 Q3	$0.177156	1,432.309	$249.33	$10	$14,323
Y7 Q4	$0.177156	1,457.683	$253.75	$10	$14,577
Y8 Q1	$0.194872	1,486.089	$284.06	$10	$14,861
Y8 Q2	$0.194872	1,515.049	$289.60	$10	$15,150
Y8 Q3	$0.194872	1,544.573	$295.24	$10	$15,445
Y8 Q4	$0.194872	1,574.672	$300.99	$10	$15,746
Y9 Q1	$0.214359	1,608.426	$337.54	$10	$16,084
Y9 Q2	$0.214359	1,642.094	$344.78	$10	$16,421
Y9 Q3	$0.214359	1,678.122	$352.17	$10	$16,781
Y9 Q4	$0.214359	1,714.094	$359.72	$10	$17,141
Y10 Q1	$0.235795	1,754.511	$404.17	$10	$17,545
Y10 Q2	$0.235795	1,795.882	$413.70	$10	$17,959
Y10 Q3	$0.235795	1,838.227	$423.46	$10	$18,383
Y10 Q4	$0.235795	1,881.572	$433.44	$10	$18,882
Y11 Q1	$0.259374	1,930.375	$488.03	$10	$19,304
Y11 Q2	$0.259374	1,980.444	$500.59	$10	$19,804
Y11 Q3	$0.259374	2,031.812	$513.68	$10	$20,318
Y11 Q4	$0.259374	2,084.512	$527	$10	$20,845
Y12 Q1	$0.285312	2,143.985	$594.74	$10	$21,440
Y12 Q2	$0.285312	2,205.156	$611.70	$10	$22,052
Y12 Q3	$0.285312	2,268.071	$629.16	$10	$22,681

(Continued)

Table 3.3   *(Continued)*

Quarter	Quarterly Dividend per Share	# of Shares Owned	Total Quarterly Dividend	Stock Price	Value
Y12 Q4	$0.285312	2,332.782	$647.10	$10	$23,328
Y13 Q1	$0.313843	2,405.995	$732.13	$10	$24,060
Y13 Q2	$0.313843	2,481.505	$755.10	$10	$24,815
Y13 Q3	$0.313843	2,559.385	$778.80	$10	$25,594
Y13 Q4	$0.313843	2,639.71	$803.24	$10	$26,397
Y14 Q1	$0.345227	2,730.84	$911.29	$10	$27,308
Y14 Q2	$0.345227	2,825.116	$942.76	$10	$28,251
Y14 Q3	$0.345227	2,922.646	$975.31	$10	$29,226
Y14 Q4	$0.345227	3,023.544	$1,008.98	$10	$30,235
Y15 Q1	$0.37975	3,138.363	$1,148.19	$10	$31,384
Y15 Q2	$0.37975	3,257.542	$1.179.91	$10	$32,575
Y15 Q3	$0.37975	3,381.247	$1,237.05	$10	$33,812
Y15 Q4	$0.37975	3,509.65	$1,284.28	$10	$35,097
Y16 Q1	$0.417725	3,656.257	$1,486.07	$10	$36,565
Y16 Q2	$0.417725	3,808.988	$1,527.30	$10	$38,099
Y16 Q3	$0.417725	3,968.099	$1,591.10	$10	$39,681
Y16 Q4	$0.417725	4,133.856	$1,657.57	$10	$41,339
Y17 Q1	$0.459497	4,323.806	$1,899.50	$10	$43,238
Y17 Q2	$0.459497	4,522.483	$1,986.78	$10	$45,225
Y17 Q3	$0.459497	4,730.29	$2,078.07	$10	$47,303
Y17 Q4	$0.459497	4,947.646	$2,173.56	$10	$49,477
Y18 Q1	$0.505447	5,197.723	$2,500.77	$10	$51,977
Y18 Q2	$0.505447	5,460.441	$2,627.14	$10	$54,604
Y18 Q3	$0.505447	5,736.437	$2,759.96	$10	$57,364
Y18 Q4	$0.505447	6,026.383	$2,899.47	$10	$60,264
Y19 Q1	$0.555992	6,361.445	$3,350.62	$10	$63,614
Y19 Q2	$0.555992	6,715.136	$3,536.91	$10	$67,151
Y19 Q3	$0.555992	7,088.492	$3,733.56	$10	$70,885
Y19 Q4	$0.555992	7,482.607	$3,941.14	$10	$74,826
Y20 Q1	$0.611591	7,940.236	$4,576.29	$10	$79,402
Y20 Q2	$0.611591	8,425.854	$4,856.18	$10	$84,259
Y20 Q3	$0.611591	8,941.171	$5,153.18	$10	$89,412
Y20 Q4	$0.611591	9,488.005	$5,468.34	$10	$94,880

Soon that becomes $2,000, then $3,000 per quarter. After 20 years, your original $10,000 investment is growing in value by $5,000 per quarter—a 200% annual return on your original investment!

So, in a flat market, through the power of reinvesting dividends, your $10,000 investment goes up more than 800% in 20 years.

Now imagine what happens if the market actually goes higher, as it typically does.

Over the past 50 years, not including dividends, the S&P 500's annual growth rate has been 7.84%.

But let's assume that the next 20 years are going to be marked by slower growth, and the market rises only by 5% annually. Using the same parameters as just described, your $10,000 turns into $26,551 after 10 years and $93,890 after 20.

It's interesting to note that after 20 years, the total is actually less than if the market had been flat. That's because by that point, the compounding dividends represent the vast majority of the position's increase, and the dividends are being reinvested at higher prices than when the market was flat.

After 10 years, though, the stock price still makes a bit of a difference because momentum of the compounded reinvested dividends is just getting started. Up until that point, the price rise of the stock is still going to contribute meaningfully to the total return.

If the market returns the 7.84% it has over the past half a century, $10,000 turns into $32,627 in 10 years and $116,855 after 20 for total returns of 226% and 1,068%, respectively.

The compounded annual growth rates equal 12.6% after 10 years and 13.1% after 20.

Compare that with the return of an S&P 500 index fund, which is how many people invest for retirement.

Over the past 10 years, if you'd invested $10,000 in the Vanguard 500 Index Fund (VFINX), you would have had $18,062 at the end of 2013. But if you'd invested in Computer Services, Inc. (Nasdaq: CVSI), a company that's been raising its dividend every year since 1971, you'd have $35,223. Reinvest the dividends and you have $22,011 for the index fund and $43,710 in Computer Services.

So far in this chapter, I've told you a lot about what should happen. Now let me show you what did happen in a few well-known stocks.

If you had purchased $10,000 worth of Colgate-Palmolive 20 years ago and reinvested the dividends, today it would be worth $133,777 and would generate $2,975 in annual income—a nearly 30% yield on your original investment.

If you'd bought it 30 years ago, your $10,000 would now be worth $892,563. Look at the difference 10 years made. And if after 30 years, you decided to stop reinvesting the dividend and collect the income instead, your annual payout would be $19,857—a 199% annual payout on your original investment.

Let's look at one more example.

In August 1994, you bought $10,000 of what would turn out to be a relatively weak performer—Coca-Cola—and reinvested the dividends. Your investment would be worth $54,917 and would generate $1,604 a year in income 20 years later. So you would be earning 16% on the bluest of the blue chips—Coca-Cola. It would be tough to get paid 16% on the worst junk bonds in the market these days.

However, watch what happens when you add another 10 years to the equation. A $10,000 purchase of Coca-Cola in 1984 is now worth $622,957.

And if you decide it's time to start cashing those checks instead of reinvesting, you can look forward to annual payouts of $18,212, an annual yield of 182% on your original investment.

Think of compounding this way: It's the money that the money you already made is making. Compounding is like a machine. And the best part is you don't have to do a darned thing once you flip the switch and turn it on. You don't have to make decisions, and it shouldn't cost you a dime.

It's simply a moneymaking device that will generate greater and greater returns every year.

Bear Markets

You may be surprised to find out that you don't need rising stock prices to make a lot of money reinvesting dividends. In fact, if your stock falls, that can be even better as it allows you to buy shares more cheaply.

For example, you buy 500 shares of a $20 stock that pays a 4.7% dividend yield and grows the dividend by 10% per year. The stock matches the S&P 500's historical average price return of 7.84%.

If you reinvest the dividends, after 10 years, your 500 shares would grow to 826 shares at a price of $42.54 per share for a total value of $35,147.

Now, instead of matching the historical average of the S&P, we encounter a sustained bear market. Since 1937, the average annual decline when the market was down for 10 years was 2.27%. That doesn't sound like much, but imagine how devastating that would be after 10 years for stocks to have lost over 20% of their value.

You, however, won't have suffered a 20%+ loss. On the contrary, your $10,000 investment would now be worth $18,452. You still would've made 84% over the 10 years, or an average compound annual growth rate of 6.3%—at a time when everyone else was sustaining losses. Plus, your investment would now be generating nearly $2,400 in income every year, a 24% yield on cost.

Because the price of your stock was declining while you were still getting paid a rising dividend, you would now own 1,160 shares, over 300 more shares than if the market had gone up 7.48%.

The crazy thing is you can actually generate very large returns even if the stock declines year after year by purchasing a stock once and reinvesting the dividend (especially when the dividend is growing).

Table 3.4 shows you how this works. We'll pick it up after year 10 as I just described, where you have 1,160 shares and the current price is $15.90. (Note: I'm adjusting the price only once per year.)

It's pretty amazing when you look at the numbers. After 20 years of a price decline that sent your shares from $20 to $12.64, your $10,000 investment is now worth $213,690. That's an average growth rate of 16.54%—all while your stock was slipping over 2% per year.

Let me point out that by the first quarter in year 15, your annual dividend yield on cost is 100%. By the third quarter of year 19, you're getting a 100% yield on your cost *per quarter.*

After 20 years, if you decide to stop reinvesting and live off the dividends, the investment will spin off over $67,000 per year, a 570% yield on your cost. Not too shabby for a $10,000 investment on a losing stock.

And keep in mind that if we were in a period when stocks were declining year after year for an extended period, chances are inflation would be quite low, or we would even be experiencing deflation. In that case, your 16% annual returns would be worth even more as far as buying power is concerned.

What a great way to protect yourself against bear markets!

Now, you may be thinking, *That's great in theory, but if we're experiencing nasty stock market declines, there's no way companies are continuing to raise their dividends.*

Data from the most recent significant market slide indicates otherwise.

According to Robert Allan Schwartz, who studied the dividend growth rates of 139 Dividend Champions during the Great Recession, 63% of the companies continued to raise their dividends in each year from 2008 to 2010.[2]

Table 3.4   Making Money Even in a Bear Market

Quarter	Quarterly Dividend per Share	# of Shares Owned	Total Quarterly Dividend	Stock Price	Value
Y11 Q1	$2.438	1,205.285	$707.53	$15.90	$19,160.14
Y11 Q2	$2.438	1,251.499	$734.86	$15.90	$19,894.80
Y11 Q3	$2.438	1,299.485	$762.83	$15.90	$20,657.62
Y11 Q4	$2.438	1,350.469	$792.07	$15.54	$20,908.77
Y12 Q1	$2.682	1,408.751	$905.47	$15.54	$21,886.24
Y12 Q2	$2.682	1,469.548	$944.54	$15.54	$22,830.78
Y12 Q3	$2.682	1,532.969	$985.31	$15.54	$23,816.09
Y12 Q4	$2.682	1,600.664	$1,027.83	$15.18	$24,303.29
Y13 Q1	$2.95	1,678.417	$1,180.54	$15.18	$25,483.03
Y13 Q2	$2.95	1,759.947	$1,237.88	$15.18	$26,721.71
Y13 Q3	$2.95	1,845.437	$1,298.01	$15.18	$28,019.73
Y13 Q4	$2.95	1,937.161	$1,361.01	$14.84	$28,744.05
Y14 Q1	$3.245	2,043.073	$1,571.59	$14.84	$30,316.33
Y14 Q2	$3.245	2,154.776	$1,657.51	$14.84	$31,973.85
Y14 Q3	$3.245	2,272.586	$1,748.13	$14.84	$33,721.98
Y14 Q4	$3.245	2,399.723	$1,843.71	$14.50	$34,800.20
Y15 Q1	$3.57	2,547.398	$2,141.54	$14.50	$36,941.75
Y15 Q2	$3.57	2,704.160	$2,273.33	$14.50	$39,215.07
Y15 Q3	$3.57	2,870.57	$2,413.23	$14.50	$41,628.30
Y15 Q4	$3.57	3,051.323	$2,561.73	$14.17	$43,245.07
Y16 Q1	$3.927	3,262.07	$2,995.34	$14.17	$46,240.41
Y16 Q2	$3.927	3,488.657	$3,202.81	$14.17	$49,443.21
Y16 Q3	$3.927	3,730.297	$3,424.65	$14.17	$52,867.87
Y16 Q4	$3.927	3,994.674	$3,661.86	$13.85	$55,329.68
Y17 Q1	$4.319	4,306.101	$4,313.52	$13.85	$59,643.15
Y17 Q2	$4.319	4,641.807	$4,649.81	$13.85	$64,292.46
Y17 Q3	$4.319	5,003.684	$5,012.31	$13.85	$69,305.27
Y17 Q4	$4.319	5,402.835	$5,403.07	$13.54	$73,135.11
Y18 Q1	$4.751	5,876.925	$6,417.03	$13.54	$79,552.60
Y18 Q2	$4.751	6,392.615	$6,980.16	$13.54	$86,553.22
Y18 Q3	$4.751	6,953.557	$7,593.15	$13.54	$94,126.37
Y18 Q4	$4.751	7,577.893	$8,259.44	$13.23	$100,249.14
Y19 Q1	$5.23	8,326.325	$9,901.13	$13.23	$110,150,27
Y19 Q2	$5.23	9,148.677	$10,879.02	$13.23	$121,029.28
Y19 Q3	$5.23	10,052.25	$11,953.48	$13.23	$132,982.77
Y19 Q4	$5.23	11,068.12	$13,134.07	$12.93	$143,098.13
Y20 Q1	$5.75	12,298.51	$15,907.33	$12.93	$159,005.66
Y20 Q2	$5.75	13,665.68	$17,675.89	$12.93	$176,681.55
Y20 Q3	$5.75	15,184.82	$19,640.84	$12.93	$196,322.39
Y20 Q4	$5.75	16,912.06	$21,824.82	$12.64	$213,690.09

I'm sure you'll recall that was a period when there was real and valid concern that our entire financial system was about to collapse. Corporate profits plunged, unemployment numbers surged, banks collapsed, and the stock market tanked, yet nearly two-thirds of the companies that had raised their dividends every year for at least 25 years continued to do so.

If you're investing for the long term, reinvesting dividends is a great way to protect and grow your portfolio during market downturns. In fact, you should almost want your stocks to fall as you're reinvesting the dividends so that you can pick up more shares cheaply. That's a little tough to withstand psychologically. No one likes to watch his or her stock go down. But if you've got the right emotional makeup and can appreciate that a lower stock price is going to help you accumulate wealth faster, as long as the stock bounces back by the time you're ready to sell in 10, 20, or 30 years, who cares where it's trading today?

How Do Bonds Compare?

Income investors like bonds because of their steady income and the reliability that investors can get their principal back when the bonds mature.

Whether we're talking about treasury, municipal, or corporate bonds, if you buy a bond, there's a very good chance you will get your money back.

Between 1925 and 2005, investment-grade bonds paid back bondholders 99.7% of the time. The default rate on higher-yielding junk bonds was 6%. So historically, junk bond investors have a 94% chance of getting their money back (although during the peak of the Great Recession, default rates in junk bonds climbed to 13%).

As I showed you earlier, during 10-year periods over the past 76 years, stocks were positive 91% of the time, about the same success ratio as junk bonds. But wait, junk bond investors *got their money back only* 94% of the time, while stock investors *made* money 91% of the time.

Furthermore, when you receive an interest payment from a bond, there is no way of making that income grow as the years go by. If you bought a 10-year corporate bond yielding 6%, you've agreed to lend the company money at a 6% interest rate.

If the company invents the next iPhone and profits explode higher, you'll receive 6%. If business is in the toilet, you'll receive 6%.

And when you get that check in the mail, the only way you're going to turn it into more money is if you find another place to invest it—an activity that's going to cost you time for sure and likely money.

If in 10 years you absolutely have to have those funds—you can't risk the money not being there—well then, you shouldn't be buying a junk bond. Invest it in a treasury.

But if you are able to take some risk, which you clearly can because you're buying a junk bond, you're better off with a stock that pays increasing dividends.

You can't reinvest bond interest. Of course, you can buy another bond if the interest payment is large enough or buy a stock or any other type of investment. But it will take time and cost you money to make another trade.

Conversely, if you're reinvesting the dividends from a stock, the dividend payment and reinvestment happen at the same time and for free with most brokers. It's one less thing that you have to think about, while your money compounds and grows.

Let's compare a junk bond and a Perpetual Dividend Raiser.

As I write this, Tesoro Corporation (NYSE: TSO) has bonds available with a 4.8% yield that mature in 10 years.

So over the next 10 years, an investor who buys $10,000 worth of bonds (10 bonds at $1,000 each) will receive annual payments totaling $480. At the end of 10 years, historically, he has a 94% chance of getting his $10,000 back and will have collected $4,800 in interest.

Also consider what happens when things go wrong. When bonds default, historically, bond investors receive only about 40% of their money back.[3]

A stock paying a 4% dividend yield whose dividend increases 10% per year would generate $6,374 in dividend payments over 10 years— more than you'd collect from the bond. And the bond price isn't going to be higher at maturity (unless you buy it below par).

The stock's price probably will be higher. Historically, it has a 91% success rate, slightly less than the bond as well. However, as I mentioned, stocks' average return is 7.84%, which *includes* down years.

After 10 years, a $10,000 investment in our example stock is worth $32,627 if dividends are reinvested. The bond plus interest is worth $14,800, less than half the amount the stock returned.

Historically, the stock has a greater chance of suffering a loss, but only by 3%. To compensate for the risk, stocks generate 92% in extra return. That's a more than acceptable reward-to-risk ratio.

And when things go wrong in the stock market—we're talking *really* wrong—stocks average a decline of 27% over 10 years. That's the historical 10-year rolling return of stocks when the market is negative over 10 years—periods associated only with the Great Depression and the Great Recession.

So in the past, you've had a 9% chance of losing 27% of your money over 10 years investing in stocks or a 6% chance of losing 40% of your money investing in high-yield bonds.

As the chapter title says, past performance does not guarantee future results. But we have decades' worth of data that shows that you have just a slightly higher chance of losing money in stocks than you do in high-yield bonds (and that's only when epic financial crises hit). And when you do lose money in stocks, you lose significantly less than you typically do with bonds.

With this information, it should be apparent that dividend stocks are a better investment than junk bonds. While the bonds may offer an attractive yield and the perception that the principal should be paid back at maturity, stocks, while a tad riskier, offer a much greater return and opportunity to generate wealth.

There will be instances when junk bonds are trading below par and offer investors the opportunity for capital gains along with the interest. However, to make the kind of gains necessary to compete with dividend stocks, the bond would have to be considered distressed, which would make it a very risky investment in most circumstances.

In those instances, it's not an apples-to-apples comparison. You'd be comparing a distressed bond versus (in all likelihood) a conservative stock—one that has a history of raising its dividend every single year. Companies in distress typically don't raise their dividends.

In fact, raising the dividend is usually a sign of financial health and confidence. Keep in mind that management would rather keep the money on the balance sheet or buy back shares, since compensation often is tied to earnings per share growth or the stock price.

When a management team raises the dividend, it signals that the company has plenty of cash to achieve its goals and expects there to be an abundance of cash in the future.

So a company with a track record of annual dividend raises that, once again, boosts its dividend is the opposite of a distressed bond.

Are You an Investor from Lake Wobegon?

Are you a good driver?

Are you a good parent? Son or daughter? Sibling? Spouse/Boyfriend/Girlfriend?

How do you rate in your, er, more intimate activities?

Most people think they're in fact pretty good in all of those categories—certainly above average. But statistics tell us that, in fact, most people cannot be above average.

And the majority of investors think they're above average in that skill, too, no matter what their brokerage statements tell them.

It reminds me of Garrison Keillor's *Prairie Home Companion,* which describes the fictional town of Lake Wobegon as a place where "all the women are strong, all the men are good-looking, and all of the children are above average."

In fact, a psychological term, the Lake Wobegon effect, is a bias in which people overestimate their abilities. Investors are notorious for this trait.

It's unlikely that you (or anyone else) are a better-than-average investor. After all, even the pros stink out the joint most of the time.

According to Standard & Poor's, the majority of actively managed (not index) mutual funds underperform their benchmark index in just about every category.[4] For the 12 months ending June 30, 2014, 60% of large-cap funds failed to return as much as the S&P 500. Mid-caps were similar with 58% of funds underperforming. And 73% of small-cap funds did not do as well as their benchmarks.

The numbers are even worse when you expand the time horizon. Over three years ending in June 2014, a staggering 85% of large-cap mutual funds underperformed. 77% of midcap funds missed their benchmarks as did a mind-blowing 92% of small-cap funds.

But wait; for large-cap and midcap funds, it gets even worse over the five-year period: 87% and 88%, respectively, performed worse than their benchmarks. Small caps improved, so to speak, to 88% underperformance.

That means investors would have been better off investing in an index fund or exchange-traded fund (ETF) that tracks the index rather than trusting the manager to beat the market.

If your money is invested in actively managed mutual funds, you are paying a fund manager to, in all likelihood, make you less money than you could have simply buying an index fund or ETF.

And according to the *Wall Street Journal,* a study conducted by Dresdner Kleinwort showed that the forecasts of investment pros "were terrible." But they found something fascinating:

> . . . an almost perfect lag between forecasts and actual results.
>
> Analysts would wait until stock prices rose and then forecast that stock prices were about to rise. After interest rates fell, analysts would forecast that interest rates were due to fall.
>
> Analysts are terribly good at telling us what has just happened but of little use in telling us what is going to happen in the future.[5]

So, if these men and women who spend 10 hours a day or more in the markets can't succeed, isn't it highly unlikely that you'll be a better stock picker than they will?

The data shows that you won't—at least when it comes to timing.

According to the DALBAR Quantitative Analysis of Investor Behavior (QAIB) study, from 1990 to 2010, the S&P 500 gained an average of 9.14% per year while the average equity fund investor saw profits of only 3.83% per year—not even enough to keep up with inflation (see Figure 3.6).

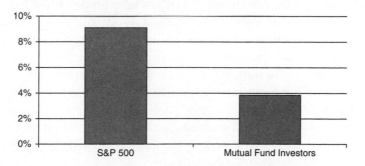

Figure 3.6 1990–2010: Equity Mutual Fund Investors' Poor Timing Leads to Subpar Results

Source: DALBAR, Inc., *Quantitative Analysis of Investor Behavior, 2011*

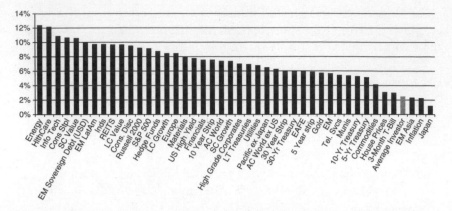

Figure 3.7 Asset Class Returns vs. The "Average Investor" 20 Years Annualized (12/31/1993–12/31/2013)

Note: Total returns in USD. Average investor is represented by Dalbar's average asset allocation, which utilizes the net of aggregate mutual.

Source: Richard Bernstein Advisors, "Toward the Sounds of Chaos," *Insights,* August 2014, www.rbadvisors.com/images/pdfs/toward_the_sounds_of_chaos.pdf

What the study in Figure 3.6 shows us is that mutual fund investors are buying and selling at the wrong times. They buy when the markets get hot and sell when they fall, the exact opposite of what they should be doing.

Need more proof? See Figure 3.7.

Figure 3.7 shows the returns of 44 sectors and asset classes over the past 20 years, including the return of the average investor. Of the 44 categories, the average investor came in 41st, mostly because of buying at market highs and selling near market lows.

Still not convinced? Figure 3.8 shows how investors pulled lots of money out at the bottom and continued to remove money from the market, failing to take advantage of the strong rebound.

The remedy is to not be an active stock picker. To be successful, buy stocks that fit the criteria in this book, and leave them alone for 10 or 20 years. Trying to trade in and out of the market is a fool's game. Do you really know when Intel is going to miss earnings or when the market is about to tank? Let me answer that. You don't. Neither do I. And neither does that lady from Goldman Sachs or that guy from Fidelity.

Invest in great companies that raise their dividends every year. In several years you will have many times more money than if you

Bad Timing

Investors pulled money out of U.S.-stock mutual funds in recent years even as stock prices climbed.

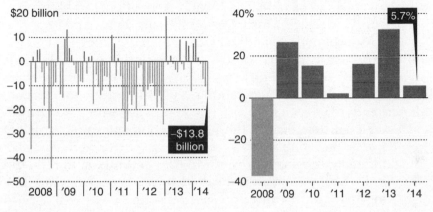

Monthly flows into and out of U.S.-stock mutual funds

S&P 500 total return

Figure 3.8 Bad Timing

Note: Data through July 31.

Source: Chart: Morgan Housel, "Three Mistakes Investors Keep Making Again and Again: Successful Investing Requires Avoiding Common Mental and Emotional Pitfalls," *Wall Street Journal*, September 12, 2014, http://online.wsj.com/articles/three-mistakes-investors-keep-making-again-and-again-1410533307; Data: Investment Company Institute (flows) and Morningstar (returns).

try to trade the market or put your investment capital in an actively managed mutual fund.

One other thing to consider in light of the fact that I just shattered your self-image as the next Warren Buffett: When you invest in dividend-paying stocks, you're often more than halfway to matching the market's return.

The market historically appreciates an average of 7.84% per year. If you own a stock with a dividend yield of 3.8%, you're just about halfway there. You don't have to be Warren Buffett. In fact, you can be a lousy stock picker, one who invests in stocks that go up only half as much as the market, and you'll match the market's performance. And if you reinvest the dividends, you'll do even better.

If you invest in a stock with a 5% yield, you only need a gain of a few percentage points during the year to beat the market and the vast majority of professional investors, including the hedge fund manager with the $20 million New York penthouse apartment, $3,000 suits, and 120-foot yacht. You'll likely beat that guy.

But investors aren't the only ones who overestimate their abilities. Some CEOs think they can generate a better return for investors instead of giving some of that cash back. And, often, they're wrong.

DePaul University's Sanjay Deshmukh and Keith M. Howe and Navigant Consulting's Anand M. Goel created a model for determining whether a CEO is "overconfident" or "rational."[6] In their research, they concluded that "an overconfident CEO pays a lower level of dividends relative to a rational CEO." Interestingly, overconfidence tends to be seen more often in companies with lower growth and lower cash flow, exactly the kind of companies where a CEO should not be overconfident.

Additionally, the market reacts with less enthusiasm to dividend announcements by companies headed by an overconfident CEO, suggesting perhaps that investors can sense the guy is a blowhard and are turned off by his management style.

Summary

- Companies that have a track record of increasing their dividend every year tend to continue raising it every year.
- Perpetual Dividend Raisers significantly outperform the market.
- The compounding of dividends is like a runaway train once it gets going and is the key to building wealth in the stock market.
- Reinvesting dividends protects you and allows you to profit in extended bear markets.
- You're not as good an investor (or driver) as you think you are. Neither are the overwhelming majority of overpaid mutual fund and hedge fund managers.

Notes

1. Aaron S. Reynolds, "The Truth About Top Performing Mutual Fund Managers," *AAII Journal*, July 2011, www.aaii.com/journal/article/the-truth-about-top-performing-mutual-fund-managers.mobile.
2. Robert Allan Schwartz, "Dividend Skeptics: Here's How Dividend Champions Fared During the Last Recession," *Seeking Alpha*, September 18, 2011, http://

seekingalpha.com/article/294269-dividend-skeptics-heres-how-dividend-champi ons-fared-during-the-last-recession.

3. Frank K. Reilly, David J. Wright, and James A. Gentry, "Historic Changes in the High Yield Bond Market," *Journal of Applied Corporate Finance* 21, no. 3 (2009): 69.

4. S&P Dow Jones Indices, *SPIVA U.S. Scorecard*, September 8, 2014, http:// us.spindices.com/resource-center/thought-leadership/spiva/.

5. Morgan Housel, "Three Mistakes Investors Keep Making Again and Again: Successful Investing Requires Avoiding Common Mental and Emotional Pitfalls," *Wall Street Journal*, September 12, 2014, http://online.wsj.com/ articles/three-mistakes-investors-keep-making-again-and-again-1410533307.

6. Sanjay Deshmukh, Anand M. Goel, and Keith M. Howe, "CEO Over-confidence and Dividend Policy," February 18, 2010, available at SSRN: http://ssrn.com/abstract=1496404 or doi:10.2139/ssrn.1496404.

Why Companies Raise Dividends

Generally speaking, management and investors have a difference of opinion on what to do with the cash on the company's balance sheet.

Management wants to keep it to use for acquisitions, for growing the company, and as a buffer against bad times. Unless a company is in its early stages or in hypergrowth mode, investors usually want to get some of that cash back—particularly if the company is growing the amount of cash flow it brings in every year.

Going back to Marc Lichtenfeld's Authentic Italian Trattoria example, if you invested in my restaurant and after a few years, we're pulling in $200,000 per year in profit, you may start to get antsy and demand some kind of payout.

I, however, may have my sights set on a new location, want to knock down a wall to expand seating, or add more staff that will help turn the tables over more quickly.

At some point, I have to balance my investors' demands with my plans for growth. Of course, if you have more money than you know what to do with, it's an easier problem to solve.

Microsoft (Nasdaq: MSFT) had $86 billion in cash and short-term investments on its books against just $23 billion in debt as of June 30, 2014. So net, it has $63 billion in cash. As they used to say in the old New York Lottery commercials, "That's a lot of bread."

Over the past three years, Microsoft has generated an average of $31 billion in cash flow from operations. Its dividend yield is 2.8%.

Despite years of huge profits and cash flow, it wasn't until 2003 that the company started paying a dividend. The $0.08 per share dividend wasn't acceptable to investors, who saw the huge stash of cash and wanted some of it returned. In 2004, with the stock price at about $24, Microsoft paid investors a dividend of $3.08 per share.

Immediately after, it went back to its $0.08 per share quarterly dividend, hiking it every year starting in 2006 to where it is now at $0.31 per share for a very respectable 14.5% compound annual growth rate.

Even still, with so much cash in the bank earning next to nothing, many shareholders believe they are entitled to some of their money back.

And thus starts one of the great arguments in investing: Who can earn a greater return on investors' money, management or shareholders?

Most management teams believe they can put the money to good use expanding their business, acquiring competitors, or buying back shares.

They contend that they can grow the money faster than an investor who receives capital back from the company.

Investors, however, argue that managements that are not making the money grow at a fast enough clip should return funds to shareholders, who can invest them in higher-growth businesses. They often feel that if management doesn't have a better use for the capital, it should give the money back to shareholders.

Buybacks versus Dividends

Rather than pay a dividend, one favorite management use of excess cash is a stock buyback—or at least the announcement of a stock buyback.

A typical buyback announcement will sound something like this:

> Company X said Thursday it plans to repurchase up to $100 million or two million shares of its common stock as part of its stock repurchase authorization through December 31, 2015.

What this means is that management, *at its discretion,* can go into the market at any time and buy its own shares. Doing so reduces the share count and increases the earnings per share (EPS).

For example, see Table 4.1. A company that earns $20 million per year and has 20 million shares outstanding will earn $1 per share ($20 million divided by 20 million shares). If it buys back two

Table 4.1   Stock Buybacks Can Increase EPS

	Net Income	EPS	P/E	Stock Price
20 million shares	$20 million	$1	15	$15
18 million shares	$20 million	$1.11	15	$16.65

million shares of stock, the $20 million in earnings is now divided by 18 million shares, which equals $1.11 per share.

Let's assume the stock trades at a price–earnings (P/E) ratio of 15. In the first scenario, it would trade at $15 (15 P/E × $1 EPS). In the second, if it maintained the 15 P/E after a buyback, it would trade at $16.65 (15 P/E × $1.11 EPS).

But here's why management teams love the share buyback program: Not only can it increase EPS, but the executives are also in complete control of the funds.

So if the economy turns south, there is a hiccup in the business, or executives simply want to hoard cash, they don't have to buy back any shares. All that they have announced is an *authorization* to repurchase stock. It doesn't mean the company has to, just that it is allowed to.

Very often, companies don't repurchase all of the stock in the plan. Then they extend the agreement when it expires. So if a company said it is authorized to buy up to $100 million worth of stock or two million shares by December 31, 2015, and it's bought only half that amount, in late 2015, it may extend the repurchase authorization to 2017 and even the amount of shares, upping it to another two million (probably knowing full well it will not purchase the entire amount). Nevertheless, the market will treat this as good news and likely give the stock a bump higher—decreasing the chance of the company actually buying back the stock, as management wants to buy its shares when they're cheap. However, will any investors complain that the stock is higher and management is not buying back shares? Probably not.

Furthermore, a buyback can be used to manipulate earnings. For example, according to *Barron's*, in January 2012, Jarden (NYSE: JAH) suspended its dividend to buy back $500 million worth of stock.[1] *Barron's* estimated that the buyback would boost earnings from $3.78 per share to $4.50.

Sounds good for the investor, right?

It does, until you take into account that Jarden's top three executives would have received huge stock grants if the company had made $4.50 per share.

So in this case, the buyback was taking money directly out of shareholders' pockets by eliminating the dividend and transferring it to management in the form of stock grants.

Over the next two years, the number of shares outstanding declined from 133 million to 115 million, a 13.5% decrease. Turns out the company never made more than $3.12 per share since the buyback was put in place. So management did not get their stock grants. Too bad.

Most buybacks aren't that sinister. But this is an example of how buybacks can be used to manipulate earnings. And keep in mind that management often receives bonuses based on EPS or EPS growth. Notice that in both the Jarden example and the earlier made-up one, the company's actual profits didn't move at all. But because there were fewer shares, the EPS rose after the buyback. It's simply an accounting trick that doesn't reflect any change in the business.

When a company pays a dividend, that's real. It's not part of an authorization plan that may or may not be executed. If a company said it's going to pay $1 per share in dividends this year, then by all means, it had better pay $1 per share in dividends—or else the stock will get crushed.

A dividend declaration is like a vote of confidence by management not only affirming that there will be enough cash to pay the dividend and run the business but also stating that it has set an expectation for a certain level of earnings and cash flow.

If it is forced to cut the dividend in the future—or, in the case of a company that has been raising the dividend year after year, to keep the dividend at the same level—the stock will be hit hard. Management knows this and recognizes that establishing or raising a dividend is akin to setting the bar at a higher level and telling shareholders that the company will at least reach that level of success.

So, management commits the company to future payouts; if it does not meet that pledge, the share price will decline.

Murali Jagannathan and Clifford P. Stephens along with Michael S. Weisbach concluded that "dividends are paid by firms with higher 'permanent' operating cash flows, while repurchases are used by firms with higher 'temporary,' non-operating cash flows."[2]

This theory was backed up in 2007 by economists Bong-Soo Lee and Oliver Meng Rui, who wrote: "We find that share repurchases are associated with temporary components of earnings, whereas dividends are not."[3]

So, according to the statement by Jagannathan, Stephens, and Weisbach, long-term investors should have more confidence in a company that pays dividends as it has more permanent operating cash flow than a company buying back shares, which is manipulating the share count to boost the EPS and possibly the price of the stock.

The share buyback is symbolic of many of the ills of today's market. Although some repurchases are done intelligently at bargain prices, for the most part they're a quick fix to lower the share count and create some positive news, even if the news isn't based in reality—because the company does not have to buy back the shares, it's only announcing that it *may* do so.

Stock buybacks, particularly with large companies, reduce the share count but may not always benefit shareholders.

Azi Ben-Rephael, Jacob Oded, and Avi Wohl, in a 2011 paper published in *Review of Finance,* determined that small companies often buy back shares at lower-than-average market prices. However, large companies do not, because large companies are "more interested in the disbursement of free cash."[4] In other words, managers of small companies attempt and succeed in repurchasing their shares at attractive prices; executives of the larger companies are more concerned with unloading excess cash and showing that they're putting it to work, under the guise of benefiting shareholders. In reality, these executives are not living up to their fiduciary duties because they are repurchasing stock at whatever the market price happens to be rather than buying back shares when they are attractively valued.

The authors concluded that when it comes to large companies, stock repurchases do not lead to better returns over the long run.

Buybacks are also used to offset employee stock option plans. If a company has 100 million shares and awards two million shares to employees (many of which go to upper management), the company may buy back two million shares to keep the outstanding shares total at 100 million. It's a way of rewarding management without diluting shareholders. When you think about it, shareholders, the owners of the company, are the ones purchasing those two million shares for the employees, so, in reality, shareholders are being diluted.

A strong dividend policy, however, is a throwback to the way our grandparents invested and ran businesses. These managers are not taking the easy way out. Instead, they commit themselves and their companies to a level of performance that its shareholders can expect year after year.

Even when times are tough, by raising dividends, management is telling shareholders they can expect an increased return every year that they own the stock.

A share buyback keeps management in control of the money. A dividend program relieves some of that control, which investors should view as a sign of capable and confident management.

Don't overlook the fact that today's management teams often own millions of shares of their companies. And while they would love for the stock price to go infinitely higher so that they can sell their shares for millions of dollars more, investors in it for the long haul also benefit from the dividend.

A CEO with one million shares of a $10 stock that pays a 4% yield receives $400,000 per year in income, which, right now, is taxed at the lower rate than his or her ordinary income rate, which is taxed significantly higher. Note that tax rates on dividends may increase at a later date. We discuss taxes in Chapter 12.

For management teams that aren't thinking about cashing out their stock anytime soon, a healthy dividend is in their best interest as well.

Critics of dividends often say companies pay a dividend because they can't come up with a better use of the money.

I disagree. There is nothing wrong with investors receiving returns on their investment every year as a reward for putting funds into a business and riding it out for the long term. Additionally, a rising dividend also instills confidence that management expects cash flows to continue to grow and puts pressure on executives to ensure that they do. You won't see many executives just punching the clock when business is tough, if they know they have to increase the amount of money they are paying out to shareholders every year.

Management Speaks

I posed this question to several executives: Why does a company adopt a policy that commits it to an ever-increasing outlay of cash in the form of dividends?

I received some interesting replies.

Scott Kingsley, the CFO of Community Bank System, Inc. (NYSE: CBU), an upstate New York bank that, as of October 2014, paid a dividend yield of 3.4% and had raised its dividend every year since 1992, said he believes the dividend keeps existing shareholders happy but also attracts new shareholders.

Regarding the idea that a company can retain capital for other uses rather than paying a dividend, he stated:

> We are very "capital efficiency" conscious. We believe "hoarding" capital to potentially reinvest via an acquisition or some other use can lead to less than desirable habits. We prefer to raise incremental capital in the market when needed—and we have a track record of doing that. Having excess capital on the balance sheet when assessing a potential use can lead to bad decisions— because at that point almost everything results in improvement to ROE [return on equity]. The case in point in our industry are the overcapitalized, converted thrifts. Their ROEs are usually so low, any transaction looks like it improves that metric, but it may not add franchise value longer term.

So, according to Kingsley, not having a stash of cash forces management to be more responsible stewards of the company's assets. When a company has lots of cash on hand and makes an acquisition, it usually increases ROE since cash, particularly these days with such low interest rates, returns practically nothing.

He is saying that you can make an acquisition that looks good as far as ROE is concerned because it returns more than cash, but in reality it doesn't do much for the business.

Return on equity (ROE): A ratio that represents the amount of profit generated by shareholders' equity. The higher the ROE, the better. The formula to calculate ROE is: net income/shareholders' equity.

Example: A company has net income of $10 million and shareholders' equity of $100 million. Its ROE is 10%.

Kingsley is absolutely right. How many boneheaded acquisitions have we seen that ultimately led a company to difficult times or even its demise?

Perhaps the most famous cash acquisition flop was the 1994 purchase of Snapple for $1.7 billion by Quaker Oats. At the time, Quaker Oats was a publicly traded company. Most on Wall Street believed that Quaker was overpaying by $1 billion.

Turns out those estimates were too conservative. In 1997, Quaker sold Snapple for just $300 million, losing $1.4 billion in three years.

The price paid equaled $25 per share of shareholders' money that was handed over to Snapple's investors.

In 2007, Clorox (NYSE: CLX) shelled out $925 million to acquire Burt's Bees so that it would gain market share in the natural products space. Apparently Clorox overpaid, as it took a $250 million impairment charge in January 2011.

Now, $250 million is small potatoes to a huge company like Clorox, but it does represent nearly $2 per share in cash, funds that I'm sure shareholders would like to have back.

When CEOs throw around millions of dollars to acquire companies, we tend not to think much of it. After all, that's why we're paying them the big bucks—to be the dealmakers, the captains of industry.

In many instances, the deals are well thought out and completed at an appropriate price. Those are situations where everyone wins in the long run.

But unfortunately, in many other cases, the Quaker Oats–Snapple or Clorox–Burt's Bees deals of the world are not unusual. And when all that money is thrown around, we tend to forget that that money belongs to shareholders. They are the owners of the company.

In 999 times out of 1,000, a company with extra cash that it might otherwise have spent on an acquisition is not going to give it back to shareholders. If Clorox hadn't bought Burt's Bees, there is no way that it would have declared a special $2 per share dividend.

But as Community Bank's Kingsley pointed out, having such a large hoard of cash can lead to decisions that do not benefit shareholders. So maybe returning some of that cash isn't such a bad idea after all.

Know Your Identity

An identity is an important part of a self-image. It often leads us to behave in a way to live up to that identity. If your identity is *the life of the party*, when you get to the party, you probably make it your business to kick it up a notch.

If your identity is to be the guy everyone can depend on in times of crisis, you step up when you see someone needs help.

I've had several identities in my life. The thoughtful and considerate guy. The hardworking, don't-have-to-worry-about-him, he'll-get-it-done guy. Now I'm the best-selling–author guy.

Companies also have identities.

Thomas Freyman, CFO of Abbott Laboratories (NYSE: ABT), told *Barron's* in February 2012, "Dividends are an important part of Abbott's investment identity and a valued component of our balanced use of strong cash flow."[5]

Abbott has paid a dividend every year since 1924 and has raised the dividend for 42 consecutive years. That's a key component of its identity. Not only does any investor who is considering becoming an Abbott shareholder take the dividend into consideration, but also it's likely an important factor in the decision of whether to invest in the company.

Attracting the Right Shareholders

Thomas Faust, CEO of money manager Eaton Vance (NYSE: EV), told me he recognizes that keeping the owners of his company happy is his job and pays off in the long run. He explained:

> Investors value dividends as an important factor in owning our stock and we have been told this firsthand by large institutional holders of Eaton Vance. You could say we benefit indirectly to the extent our stock has a higher valuation because of our long record of dividend increases.

Eaton Vance has grown its dividend every year since 1980, including a 50% increase in 2003, when the dividend tax rate dropped to 15%. That had to have made shareholders very happy. (See Figure 4.1.)

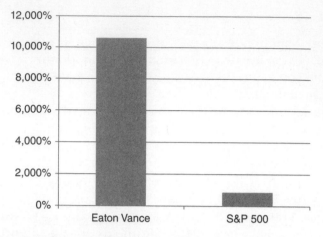

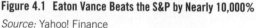

Figure 4.1 Eaton Vance Beats the S&P by Nearly 10,000%
Source: Yahoo! Finance

Clearly it did. Over the past 25 years, when dividends are reinvested, Eaton Vance's stock outperformed the S&P 500 by over 9,780%!

As Freyman and Faust appreciate, a dividend that is consistently climbing keeps existing shareholders happy and attracts new ones.

Stocks that have a lot of momentum and whose price is rising rapidly also attract new shareholders, but are they the *right* shareholders?

Ultimately, management wants long-term investors as owners of the company. These investors will typically be those who understand the big picture and won't get bent out of shape if the company's earnings fail to meet expectations one quarter. They will likely be more patient shareholders than those who are in it for a quick buck.

Investors usually understand the company's business. As long as there has been no fundamental change to the business, shareholders will stay invested, particularly if they are receiving a growing dividend.

Other investors with a shorter time horizon often bail out of a stock that fails to meet earnings expectations during a quarter. Stocks that miss analysts' estimates frequently fall in price immediately after the earnings report is released, triggering a stampede out of the stock.

But shareholders who do not panic have the opportunity to buy more shares or reinvest their dividends at a lower price as a result.

Investors who have owned shares for years are likely satisfied with their returns (and yield); otherwise they would no longer be shareholders. Managements and boards of directors have a vested interest in keeping long-term shareholders satisfied. If those investors are happy, management and the board members probably get to keep their jobs.

When shareholders are not content, people get fired. Occasionally, you will see a group of investors so unhappy that they attempt to vote out the board of directors or force the CEO and other executives to resign.

That was the case in 2014 when Darden's (NYSE: DRI) CEO was forced to resign and shareholders voted to replace the entire board of directors after years of slow growth and a sale of assets that was not in shareholders' best interests.

This group of investors who force change at a company are called activist investors. They are usually hedge funds that own a big stake in the company and recruit others to vote along with them to make substantial modifications.

Activist investor: An investor that owns 5% or more of a company's outstanding shares and files a 13D document with the Securities and Exchange Commission. The 13D lets the company and the public know that the investor may demand or is demanding changes from management or the board.

Management wants to avoid getting into a battle with activist investors for several reasons.

It can be expensive to counter the activist's arguments. An activist may issue press releases, hire attorneys, and demand a vote to make changes within the company.

Countering those activist moves can cost millions of dollars.

Additionally, activists occasionally resort to public humiliation of a CEO or board to achieve their goals.

In 2011, for example, Dan Loeb, a noted activist investor, wrote a letter to the board of directors of Yahoo! (Nasdaq: YHOO) demanding the resignation of cofounder Jerry Yang after Yang had engaged in negotiations to sell the company.

In the letter, Loeb stated:

> More troubling are reports that Mr. Yang is engaging in one-off discussions with private equity firms, presumably because it is in his best personal interests to do so. The Board and the Strategic Committee should not have permitted Mr. Yang to engage in these discussions, particularly given his ineptitude in dealing with the Microsoft negotiations to purchase the Company in 2008; it is now clear that he is simply not aligned with shareholders.[6]

As you can imagine, these kinds of letters don't do much for the reputation of Yang or the rest of the board. So a company generally does not want to get into an altercation with an activist.

By the way, Loeb succeeded. Yang resigned from the board of directors in January 2012. Today, other than being a shareholder, Yang no longer has a relationship with the company he started.

What does all of this have to do with investing in dividend stocks?

Normally, a company that is paying a healthy dividend and lifting that dividend year after year doesn't incur the wrath of angry shareholders. Investors who buy stocks with 4%+ yields that grow every year by 10% are typically doing so because of the income opportunities. As long as the dividend program remains intact at the levels the investors expect, they probably will stay quiet, let management do its job, and collect dividend checks every quarter.

Additionally, if a management team has a dividend policy, such as the one just described, chances are, it's running a shareholder-friendly company. Executives who are committed to increasing the dividend every year are more likely to take seriously their fiduciary responsibilities to shareholders than executives who are simply focused on jacking up the quarterly earnings numbers.

Once in a while you get an activist situation that demands a special dividend, particularly when a company is sitting on a lot of cash and there aren't any attractive acquisition opportunities.

But those are usually companies that are paying very small dividends or none at all.

Even a company with a war chest of cash usually will not come under pressure from shareholders if it pays a solid dividend that grows every year.

Although the yield is very important, serious dividend investors consider the safety of the dividend (the likelihood it will get paid) to be just as important. So they won't force a company to blow a large chunk of its cash in order to push the dividend yield through the roof. They'll be happy as long as the dividend is growing at a respectable pace year after year.

Dividend investors tend to be rational; they understand the logic in how much of a dividend is paid as well as the reasons to invest in these stable, "boring" companies rather than chase the next big thing.

Signals to the Market

When companies report their quarterly earnings results, the language they use is couched in legal speak and cautionary statements. Companies never want to set expectations too high because when they fail to meet those prospects, the stocks get punished.

Additionally, when things are not going great, management will try to use more optimistic language to dilute the bad news.

But a raised dividend says more than a CEO can ever state. Generally speaking, it says: We have enough cash to pay shareholders a higher dividend, and *we expect to generate more cash to continue to sustain a growing dividend.*

As economists Merton H. Miller and Franco Modigliani point out, when "a firm has adopted a policy of dividend stabilization with a long-established and generally appreciated 'target payout ratio,' investors are likely to (and have good reason to) interpret a change in the dividend rate as a change in management's views of future profit prospects for the firm."[7] They were the first economists to suggest that dividend policy is an indication of executives' beliefs on the prospects of their companies.

The University of Chicago's Douglas J. Skinner and Harvard University's Eugene F. Soltes agree, writing: "We find that the reported earnings of dividend-paying firms are more persistent than those of other firms and that this relation is remarkably stable over time. We also find that dividend payers are less likely to report losses and those losses that they do report tend to be transitory losses driven by special items."[8]

In the same paper, the two professors concur with the earlier statements that stock buybacks do not convey the same confidence as dividends because they represent "less of a commitment than dividends."

Especially for companies with track records of five years or more of raising dividends, the higher dividend not only delivers a higher income stream to shareholders, it also sends a clear message that the policy of raising dividends is intact and should be for the foreseeable future.

A higher dividend is certainly not a guarantee that the dividend will get a boost next year. But it is a good indication that management is serious about the policy and will likely work to ensure it can be maintained.

The growth in the dividend is especially noteworthy during a disappointing earnings period. As I mentioned, when a company misses earnings expectations, investors sometimes panic, which can lead to management getting unnerved and making drastic decisions, such as layoffs and restructurings.

But when earnings are not so hot and the company still raises the dividend, the message is that things are not so bad. It's as if management is telling you, "There is still plenty of cash on the books, and it's likely that we'll generate enough cash next year to raise the dividend again."

For an investor looking at the big picture, that's a powerful message. The chatter may be about the near-term disappointment; the shareholder who's in it for the long haul and understands that businesses go through cycles of ups and downs sees that the company's strategy is intact and should be able to weather the storm.

The market gets this message loud and clear. Companies that raise dividends year after year tend to outperform the market. As I showed you in Chapter 3, the Perpetual Dividend Raisers historically outperform the market.

And keep in mind that most of the Perpetual Dividend Raisers are what you might describe as stodgy, old companies. They aren't high-growth tech companies that will benefit from some hot new technology or trend.

The market clearly appreciates the fact that these companies are strong enough to raise their dividend payment every year.

Summary

- Dividends represent a stronger commitment to shareholders than stock buybacks.
- Companies that pay dividends have higher-quality cash flow.

- Management teams that take their fiduciary duty seriously act responsibly with the company's cash.
- A raised dividend signals management's confidence in the company's prospects.
- Jarden's executives like money more than their shareholders.

Notes

1. Michael Santoli, "Follow Up," *Barron's*, January 30, 2012, 18.
2. Murali Jagannathan, Clifford P. Stephens, and Michael S. Weisbach, "Financial Flexibility and the Choice between Dividends and Stock Repurchases," *Journal of Financial Economics* 57 (2000): 355.
3. Bong-Soo Lee and Oliver Meng Rui, "Time-Series Behavior of Share Repurchases and Dividends," *Journal of Financial and Quantitative Analysis* 42 (2007): 119–142, doi:10.1017/S0022109000002210.
4. Azi Ben-Rephael, Jacob Oded, and Avi Wohl, "Do Firms Buy Their Stock at Bargain Prices? Evidence from Actual Stock Repurchase Disclosures," *Review of Finance* 18, no. 4 (2014): 1299–1340, doi: 10.1093/rof/rft028.
5. Shirley A. Lazo, "Four Times the Fun: Fidelity National Quadruples Dividend, Boosts Stock," *Barron's*, February 18, 2012, http://online.barrons.com/news/articles/SB50001424052748703786004577221390164129740.
6. Third Point, "Third Point Requests Two Yahoo Board Seats, Demands Yang's Resignation from Board, and Opposes Reported Negotiations for 'Sweetheart' Deal with Private Equity Firms," news release, November 4, 2011, www.businesswire.com/news/home/20111104006045/en/Point-LLC-Letter-Yahoo!-Board-Directors.
7. Merton H. Miller and Franco Modigliani, "Dividend Policy, Growth, and the Valuation of Shares," *Journal of Business* 34 (October 1961): 430.
8. Douglas J. Skinner and Eugene F. Soltes, "What Do Dividends Tell Us About Earnings Quality?" Abstract, *Review of Accounting Studies* 16, no. 1 (March 2011), http://ssrn.com/abstract=484542.

Get Rich with Boring Dividend Stocks (Snooze Your Way to Millions)

How Much Do You Want to Make?

If you're an investor who needs income now, I've shown you how you can double your yield within 10 years by owning stocks that grow their dividends by 10% per year every year.

The increasing yield on cost should stay ahead of the pace of inflation and, if inflation doesn't get too ugly, put a little extra in your pocket as well.

But where this method of investing really gets exciting is when you reinvest the dividends.

We'd all *like* more income today. But if you're an investor who doesn't *need* the income right away and can put off instant gratification for long-term benefits, reinvesting your dividends can generate the kinds of returns you probably thought were impossible.

For example, you can triple your money in 10 years owning stocks that go up less than the market average.

A stock with a 5% yield that grows its dividend by an average of 10% and whose price rises 6%, below the 7.84% long-term average of the S&P 500, generates a compound annual growth rate of 12.34% over 10 years. An investment of $10,000 turns into $32,028.

Just five years later, that $32,028 nearly doubles to $62,754; it more than doubles again five years later to $132,757 for a compound annual growth rate of 13.8% and a total return of 1,227%.

So, for those of you who have 20 years, a $100,000 investment today would be worth $1.32 million in 20 years.

The dividend reinvestment strategy gets its power from compounding dividends. The concept of compounding is something that should be taught in elementary schools. We would be a much more financially literate country if our kids understood the concept from a young age.

Perhaps savings would start earlier. Maybe we wouldn't let our credit card debt get out of hand if we understood how compounding works—that each period's interest is piled on top of interest, which generates even more interest (or dividends).

It's not surprising that the financially illiterate suffered greatly during the financial meltdown of 2008.

Many studies have shown that lack of financial literacy leads to lower net worth and the likelihood of being unprepared for retirement.

You don't need to be able to make decisions based on yield curves, standard deviations, or an investment's beta. But you'd better have a clear understanding of basic concepts so that when a broker or financial planner makes a recommendation, you'll have a sense of whether it's the right move for you or whether he's just getting paid a fat commission to put you into that specific product.

Many well-educated people are so scared of what they don't know financially that they simply turn their money over to someone to manage and just nod blankly at her recommendations—sometimes because they don't want to look foolish or admit that they don't know something.

I know plenty of smart people, with master's degrees and doctorates, who blindly follow whatever their broker tells them.

You may have a wonderful advisor who does a terrific job, but you should know exactly why the advisor is taking the steps that she is with your money.

Once you grasp and apply the concept of compounding early in life, the road to financial independence begins.

When I first got out of school, I learned something about saving for retirement that helped me quite a bit. A 21-year-old who invests $2,000 in an individual retirement account for 10 years and then stops investing new money will make more than someone who starts at 31 and continues investing until he's 60. That's staggering when you think about it but is accurate due to the power of compounding.

So, I did begin investing when I was young, investing in mutual funds like you're supposed to do. I left my financial future up to the professionals. These guys went to the best schools, had well-paying jobs, and were written up in all of the investing magazines. Surely they would secure my retirement for mc.

As I showed you in Chapter 3, this wasn't the best move I could make as actively managed mutual funds fail miserably at achieving average market returns. According to Vanguard's legendary founder, John Bogle, from 1984 to 2003, stock mutual funds returned an average annual return of 9.3% versus the S&P 500, which returned 12.2%.

You'd be better off buying the SPDR S&P 500 ETF (NYSE: SPY), which tracks the S&P 500, and leaving it alone for 40 years, rather than letting one of these guys get their paws on your money.

It's not that the fund managers are stupid. They're not. Beating the market is a very tough game to play. And sometimes fund managers trade too much or have to turn over their portfolio too often. Plus, you're usually paying at least 1% in expenses just for them to hold and manage your money.

If that money were invested in some dividend-paying stocks held in a discount brokerage, you would pay about $10 to buy each stock and then nothing at all after that. No 1% of your assets each year being siphoned off to a fund manager or financial advisor. How much would that 1% per year add up to if you paid that out for 20 years? More than 20% of your original investment because of the power of compounding.

Assuming you have a $100,000 mutual fund portfolio that actually beats its peers and tracks the S&P 500, and has a low 1% expense ratio, after 20 years your portfolio would be worth $346,000, and you would have shelled out over $41,000 in fees. That's money that should be yours for your retirement. It shouldn't go to the manager of the Fidelity XYZ Fund or to Dave from Merrill Lynch, who set up your portfolio and doesn't do much else for you other than sending you a Christmas card in December.

Table 5.1 shows the difference between a mutual fund that performs at the market average, with the S&P's average dividend yield over the past 50 years of 3.16% (about a full percentage point higher than today's yield), with the long-term average dividend growth rate of 5.6%, that takes a 1% management fee each year versus a portfolio of 10 dividend stocks (the kind we use in the 10–11–12 System) with an average 4% yield, 10% dividend growth, average market performance, and no management fee, with dividends reinvested.

Table 5.1   How Much Can You Save?

	Investment	Fees (20 Years)	Total $ (5 Years)	Total $ (10 Years)	Total $ (20 Years)
10 dividend stocks	$10,000	$100 ($10 commission × 10 trades)	$17,873	$32,627	$116,855
Mutual fund	$10,000	$6,097	$16,086	$25,499	$61,655

The expenses of mutual funds are a hidden cost because you don't actually see the money taken out of your account. Rather, the expense fees hurt performance. So if your fund's holdings went up 6% in value during the year but the fund has a 1% expense ratio, your return would be only 4.94%. (If the account value started at $100,000 and grew by 6% to $106,000, and management took a 1% fee, the portfolio would be left with $104,940.)

Even worse is if you're paying a financial advisor 1% per year. That's money that actually does come out of your account and is no longer available to invest.

If you have a $500,000 account, growing at 10% per year, after 10 years, you've paid over $83,000. Of course, if your advisor is helpful in planning for retirement, your kids' education, insurance products, asset allocation advice, and the like, and his or her advice makes you an extra $84,000 over that time or enables you to sleep at night, it will be worth paying the yearly management fee.

But if all your broker does is peddle you stock opportunities, stick you in some underperforming or index funds, or execute your ideas, you're better off investing with a discount broker and keeping those fees for yourself, so they can compound over the years to make you even more money.

Let's assume that instead of paying out the $83,000 in fees over 10 years, you invested with a discount broker.

Growing at 10% per year, your money would increase to $1,296,871 after 10 years and no fees versus $1,172,867 if you paid your advisor 1% per year. That's a difference of over $124,000. So it's not just the $83,000 you're paying to the advisor; it's also costing you another $40,000 in profits.

I don't want to make it sound like I'm totally against financial planners. A good one who helps you achieve your financial goals better than you can do it yourself is worth what you're paying him or her. But there are many who are merely salespeople who happen to sell financial products. Those people are not worth the fees you pay them. In some cases, they're not even looking out for your best interests. They're selling you the products that will land them the largest commissions. Invested wisely, the money that you pay them, in your pocket instead, can add substantially to your returns.

So, how much money do you want to make? Do you want to double your investment? Triple it? It's up to you. Of course, the higher gains that you shoot for, the more risk you take on, but that risk is relative. We're not talking about biotech penny stocks that can implode and go to zero on some bad news.

We're talking about companies that have a long history of paying and raising dividends, whose management teams would like to keep that record intact.

Of course, anything can happen. The markets can swoon; a particular stock can dive on a missed earnings report or scandal. But for the most part, we're talking solid companies with good track records. And even if the stock does slide, if the dividend continues to be raised, that's an opportunity to buy more stock.

So let's take a look at some ways to make boatloads of money without having to do a whole lot of work.

In Table 5.2, you can see various assumptions. We're going to adjust for initial yield, dividend growth, and stock price growth. We'll assume the initial investment was $10,000.

This table drives home the point about how powerful compounding dividends is. Notice how the end result after 20 years is higher if the dividend growth rate is higher as opposed to the stock price growth.

For example, if you bought a stock with a 5% yield and 10% dividend growth rate, and the stock price increased just 1% per year, the stock would be worth over $145,000 after 20 years.

However, if the stock price increased 5% per year, you'd wind up with about $128,000, a *lower* value.

That doesn't seem like it should make sense, that a stock growing at a faster pace would have a lower value after 20 years.

But you have to consider that for all of those 20 years of reinvesting the dividend, you end up with many more shares of the slower-growth stock. Because the stock price is lower and the dividend is rising, you can buy more shares each quarter. Over time, all of those shares add up.

Table 5.2 How Much Money Do You Want to Make?

Initial Yield	Dividend Growth Rate	Stock Price Growth	Value After 5 Years	Value After 10 Years	Value After 20 Years	Time to Double(years)	Time to Triple (years)
4%	8%	1%	$13,199	$19,062	$60,732	10.75	14.75
4%	10%	1%	$13,320	$20,104	$89,294	10	13.75
4%	8%	5%	$15,716	$25,484	$75,049	8	12
4%	10%	5%	$15,842	$26,551	$93,890	7.75	11.25
4%	8%	8%	$17,862	$31,908	$101,815	6	10
4%	10%	8%	$17,994	$33,013	$118,654	6	9.75
5%	8%	1%	$13,967	$21,821	$90,200	9.25	13
5%	10%	1%	$14,126	$23,317	$145,504	8.75	12
5%	8%	5%	$16,549	$28,479	$97,118	7	11
5%	10%	5%	$16,716	$29,972	$128,348	7	10.25
5%	8%	8%	$18,751	$35,161	$123,631	6	9
5%	10%	8%	$18,923	$36,685	$149,619	6	9

78

How many more shares do you get at the lower stock price growth rate?

If the stock increases just 1% per year, you'd have 11,924 shares (after starting with just 1,000). The stock that grows 5% per year results in a total of 4,837 shares, less than half the number of shares than the 1% grower.

At the higher growth rate, you'd have 4,837 shares of stock at a price of $26.53, whereas the 1% grower gives you 11,924 shares at $12.20.

As the price of the stock experiences higher levels of growth, the price does in fact make an important contribution to the end value.

But, as you can see, if you're in a long-term dividend reinvestment program, the starting yield and dividend growth rate are just as important, if not more so, than the growth rate of the stock itself.

In fact, the best thing that could happen to you would be for the stock to languish for a long time while you continue to buy cheap shares. Then at some point in the distant future (preferably when you're getting ready to sell), the stock takes off and achieves some measure of growth.

Even if your stock doesn't move much over the years but continues to raise the dividend at a healthy clip and run a successful business, you shouldn't worry about it.

It could wind up being the best thing that ever happened to you because you grow the number of shares you own significantly, which will generate more dividends to reinvest or spend as income.

Keep in mind that you don't have to sell your shares to reap the benefits. Let's say you've successfully reinvested your dividends for 20 years in the stock with the 5% initial yield and 10% dividend growth but just 1% growth.

After the 20-year period, you need the income from the stock and stop reinvesting the dividends to collect them. At that point, the stock is paying a yield of 30.6% per year on your original cost, and your $10,000 investment generates $8,578 per *quarter* in dividend income, or $34,312 per year for an annual yield of over 343% on your original investment.

If, instead, the stock price grew 5% per year, it still yields 30.6% on your original cost, but because you were able to buy fewer shares all those years (because the price was higher), your quarterly income is $3,594—or $14,376 per year. Still not bad at all on a $10,000 investment, particularly one that is now worth 13 times what you originally paid for it.

Now, I'm not suggesting you try to find stocks that are going to be duds in order to accumulate more shares. As you can see, there is a point where the increase in the stock price does make a difference to your total return.

But I wanted to point out that huge things can happen even if your stock is a disappointment as far as price, as long as it grows the dividend by a meaningful amount every year.

As I stated at the beginning of this book, the way we approach stocks seems to have changed over the past 15 years. We've become a society of stock traders who agonize over every tick rather than investors in good companies that are in them for the long term.

And the fact that your stock may be as boring as a high school trigonometry class could be a good thing. According to a study by Harvard Business School's Malcolm Baker, Acadian Asset Management's Brendan Bradley, and New York University's Jeffrey Wurgler, between 1968 and 2002, "Low-volatility and low-beta portfolios offered an enviable combination of high average returns and small drawdowns."[1]

Beta: A measure of volatility or risk. It is the correlation of a stock's or portfolio's change in value in response to a move by the overall market. A stock with a beta of 1 will move exactly the way the broad market moves. A stock with a beta of 0.5 would result in a price change that is half of the market's. A stock with a beta of 2 would be double the market's move.

Example: Stock A has a beta of 1, Stock B has a beta of 0.5, and Stock C has a beta of 2. They all trade at $10. If the stock market rises 10%, Stock A should climb 10% and trade at $11. Stock B only goes up 5% to trade at $10.50. Stock C jumps 20% to trade at $12.

According to the study, $1 invested in 1968 in the quintile of lowest-volatility stocks was worth $59.55 in 2002. This contrasts with a result of just $0.58 for stocks with the highest volatility.

This concept runs counter to what we've always been led to believe—that to reap outsized gains we need to take on additional risk, and that boring stocks produce boring returns.

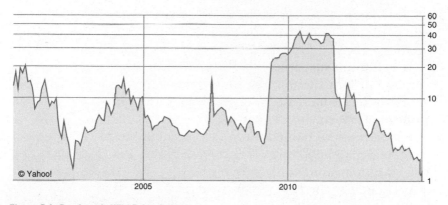

Figure 5.1 Dendreon's Wild Price Swings
Source: Yahoo! Finance

Dividend-paying stocks are often considered boring stocks. Insurance companies, real estate investment trusts, big consumer products companies, and utilities don't have the sizzle of the hottest new technology or biotech stocks. And, of course, everyone can point to the companies that were enormously successful, such as Google (Nasdaq: GOOG) and Apple (Nasdaq: AAPL). But for every one of those, there are many, many companies, like Real Networks (Nasdaq: RNWK), that have never consistently made money and whose shareholders have taken a beating.

Consider a high-beta company like Dendreon (Nasdaq: DNDN) with a beta of nearly 4 (see Figure 5.1). Over the past 10 years, Dendreon's stock price has been all over the place, possibly making fortunes for investors or traders lucky enough to be on the right side of the trade but also losing gobs of money for those who got it wrong.

In comparison, the S&P 500 Dividend Aristocrats index has a beta of 0.91, which means its price change should be only 91% of that of the S&P 500.

Table 5.3 shows a list of some "boring" Aristocrats/Champions and their betas.

Now let's look at Table 5.4, which shows these same boring stocks and how they have performed over the past 10 years. Note that this list is price only, not including dividends.

As you can see, some of these boring stocks outperformed the S&P 500, of which they're a part.

Table 5.3   Aristocrats/Champions and Their Betas

Company	Beta
Coca-Cola (NYSE: KO)	0.41
Consolidated Edison (NYSE: ED)	−0.02
ExxonMobil (NYSE: XOM)	0.89
Illinois Tool Works (NYSE: ITW)	1.15
Kimberly-Clark (NYSE: KMB)	0.04
McDonald's (NYSE: MCD)	0.45
Procter & Gamble (NYSE: PG)	0.35
Wal-Mart (NYSE: WMT)	0.34
S&P 500	1.00

Source: Yahoo! Finance

Now, when we include reinvested dividends, look what happens (see Table 5.5).

Going back to my earlier idea that investors became traders in the late 1990s and seemed to have forgotten how to invest for the long haul, somehow the notion of a 10% to 15% annual return isn't sexy anymore. They want to double or triple their money on the next great stock.

Believe me, I like a good speculation as much as the next guy. And I absolutely love researching tiny biotech companies that could be the next 5 or 10 bagger (a stock that goes up 5 or 10 times the original investment).

But those trades are for the money that you'd take to Vegas. That's not investing unless you really know something about the company that Wall Street does not. And even then, they're a big risk.

Table 5.4   Low Beta Doesn't Mean Poor Performance

Company	Beta	Performance
Coca-Cola (NYSE: KO)	0.41	87%
Consolidated Edison (NYSE: ED)	−0.02	37%
ExxonMobil (NYSE: XOM)	0.89	115%
Illinois Tool Works (NYSE: ITW)	1.15	93%
Kimberly-Clark (NYSE: KMB)	0.04	65%
McDonald's (NYSE: MCD)	0.45	246%
Procter & Gamble (NYSE: PG)	0.35	48%
Wal-Mart (NYSE: WMT)	0.34	43%
S&P 500	1.00	81%

Source: Yahoo! Finance

Table 5.5   Reinvested Dividends Provide Great Returns in Low-Beta Stocks

Company	Beta	Total Return
Coca-Cola (NYSE: KO)	0.42	147%
Consolidated Edison (NYSE: ED)	0.27	124%
ExxonMobil (NYSE: XOM)	0.53	170%
Illinois Tool Works (NYSE: ITW)	1.10	143%
Kimberly-Clark (NYSE: KMB)	0.34	134%
McDonald's (NYSE: MCD)	0.34	368%
Procter & Gamble (NYSE: PG)	0.47	95%
Wal-Mart (NYSE: WMT)	0.43	77%
S&P 500	1.00	123%

Source: Yahoo! Finance

If you don't think that an annual return of 10% to 15% is solid, you'll never be satisfied. You're the guy who goes out to a great meal and complains that the valet took too long to get your car. You're the woman who's married to the handsome prince and complains about his mother.

Look at Table 5.6 and see what you can do with an average return of 10% to 15% per year.

Impressive numbers, right? As Tom Petty sang, "The waiting is the hardest part."

It's tough to get those double-digit returns, particularly the ones north of 13%, after just five years. For example, if you buy a stock with a 5% dividend that has 10% annual dividend growth and 5% stock price appreciation, after five years your average compounded annual growth rate will be 10.82%. Because of the power of compounding, that average annual growth rate rises to 11.60% over 10 years and 13.61% over 20.

Table 5.6 $100,000 Turns into . . .

Starting Amount	Average Annual Return	5 Years	10 Years	20 Years	Years to $1 Million
$100,000	10%	$161,051	$259,374	$672,750	
$100,000	11%	$168,505	$283,942	$806,231	
$100,000	12%	$176,234	$310,584	$964,629	
$100,000	13%	$184,283	$339,456	$1,152,308	19
$100,000	14%	$192,541	$370,722	$1,374,348	18
$100,000	15%	$201,135	$404,555	$1,636,653	17

In this scenario, your $100,000 would turn into $1 million after 18.75 years.

That may sound like a long time, but if you're in your forties, fifties, or sixties, think about where you were 19 years ago. The time sure flies, doesn't it?

Wouldn't it have been nice to have put away a sum of money back then and forgotten about it, only to see it worth more than 10 times what you invested?

I was working my first job out of college at a credit union 19 years ago. I wasn't making much money, but because I had worked since I was 12 years old and was always a good saver, I had some money to invest.

If I had put away $25,000 into a quality dividend stock back then, today I'd likely have my eighth grader's college paid for.

If everyone did this when his or her children were born, rather than handing investments over to some mutual fund manager who will underperform the market or trying to pick hot stocks, chances are when those kids are ready for college, most if not all of the needed funds will be there.

Events two decades away seem impossible to fathom now but will get here sooner than you think.

College, a wedding, retirement, traveling around the world, setting up a new business—are all things that can be achieved by starting this kind of program today and not touching the money for 18 to 20 years.

Admittedly, that's not easy for most of us. When things are that far away and that expensive, they are daunting.

When my son was born, I was told it would cost roughly $80,000 per year for him to go to college. We started saving for him immediately, but still, the idea that we would have to come up with $320,000 and then another $320,000 (and likely more) for my daughter a few years later made us want to not even think about it.

And keep in mind that what I've shown you are the results of just investing once and letting the dividends compound. If, occasionally, you had some spare cash to invest and bought more stock, the results would be even greater. You don't need to have a huge amount to make a difference.

If your starting purchase is $2,500 and every few months you buy $200 more worth of stock, or whatever you can afford, that money will also compound over the years and turn into significantly more.

So although this chapter is all about the ease of the system, you can step on the gas once in a while with any extra funds that you can afford to invest. I strongly encourage you to do so when you're able.

Our consumer culture has turned us into instant-gratification hogs. We want it all and we want it now. The idea of putting off enjoyment or letting our money sit and work for us for 19 years or so is a foreign concept for many of us.

Particularly when we are being bombarded all day by marketing messages telling us we have to have the latest car, TV, and gadget.

I've already told you that I'm not going to try to turn you into a saver if you're not. That's above my pay grade. It's all on you.

What I hope I've been able to show you in this chapter is what you can accomplish if you do save and invest.

Essentially, your financial dreams *can* come true. All it takes is to put some money away and invest it in quality companies that pay a decent yield and grow the dividend every year by a meaningful amount.

Summary

- Boring, low-beta stocks outperform over the long term.
- You can triple your money in 10 years even if the market goes up less than its historical average.
- Your portfolio can rise 1,000% in 20 years using the 10–11–12 System.
- With a 13% average annual total return, $100,000 turns into $1 million in 19 years.
- You may be flushing thousands of dollars down the toilet by paying an advisor who doesn't make more money for you than he's making from you.

Note

1. Malcolm Baker, Brendan Bradley, and Jeffrey Wurgler, "Benchmarks as Limits to Arbitrage: Understanding the Low-Volatility Anomaly," *Financial Analysts Journal* 67, no. 1 (2011): 40.

CHAPTER 6

Get Higher Yields
(and Maybe Some Tax Benefits)

Certain types of stocks pay higher yields than your typical dividend stock. These include closed-end funds, real estate investment trusts (REITs), business development companies (BDCs), master limited partnerships (MLPs), and preferred stocks. While these types of stocks are lesser known and can be a little more complicated, they are worthy of your consideration. Additionally, MLPs have unique tax implications.

Let's start with the simplest: closed-end funds.

Buying $1 in Assets for $0.90

You're probably familiar with mutual funds. Those are investments where your funds are pooled with other investors' money and the fund manager buys a portfolio of stocks, bonds, or other assets. The price of the fund is equal to the value of the assets in the fund divided by the number of outstanding shares.

For example, if the Marc Lichtenfeld Dividend and Income fund (which I operate out of Marc Lichtenfeld's Authentic Italian Trattoria's back office) has $10 million under management and there are one million shares outstanding, the fund is worth $10 per share ($10 million/one million shares = $10). If tomorrow the stock market rises, the value of the assets goes up to $10.5 million, and the share count remains the same, the fund will be priced at $10.50 per share ($10.5 million/one million shares = $10.50).

Anyone who wants to own the fund buys it directly from the fund company and pays $10.50 per share. The mutual fund company will create new shares as a result of the purchase. The price per share will not change because the price now reflects the new money that just came into the fund.

For example, a buyer purchases $100,000 worth of fund shares at $10.50 per share. That means the buyer buys 9,523.8 shares ($100,000/$10.50 = 9,523.8). The fund, which had $10.5 million in it, now has $10.6 million because of the $100,000 of new money that the investor gave to the fund.

The Marc Lichtenfeld Dividend and Income fund now has $10.6 million in assets divided by 1,009,523.8 shares (the original 1,000,000 shares plus the newly created 9,523.8 shares). The price per share remains $10.50 ($10.6 million/1,009,523.8 shares = $10.50).

Anyone who wants to sell will also get $10.50 per share from the fund company, and those shares will be removed from the share count as a result. The price of the fund fluctuates exactly with the price of the assets in the fund.

A closed-end fund is a little different. A closed-end fund is essentially a mutual fund with an important difference: It trades like a stock. Its price is determined by supply and demand for the fund itself, not entirely by the price of the assets.

The price of the assets will have an effect on the demand for the fund but is not the sole determining factor in the price, the way it is with mutual funds. Therefore, it's possible (and usual) that the price of the fund will be lower (a discount) or higher (a premium) than the value of the assets rather than equal to the asset value.

Like a stock, when a person buys a closed-end fund, she is buying it from another party, not from the fund company. This contrasts with a mutual fund, where investors can only buy shares newly created by the fund company for purchase.

Premium: The price an investor pays that is higher than the actual value of the fund's assets.

Discount: The price an investor pays that is lower than the actual value of the fund's assets.

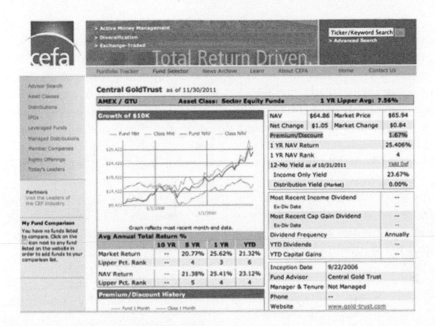

Figure 6.1 Closed-End Funds Association Site

Source: Closed End Fund Association and Lipper, a Thomson Reuters Company

When researching a closed-end fund, you always want to know whether it is trading at a premium or discount to its net asset value (NAV)—the value of the assets in the fund.

To find the NAV, you usually have to go to a site that focuses on closed-end funds or one that has a section dedicated to them. You won't find NAVs on Yahoo! Finance or in the stock quotes in your newspaper. (See Figure 6.1.)

I usually go to the website of the Closed-End Fund Association (CEFA; www.cefa.com). The CEFA is a trade organization for closed-end funds, and the website has a lot of useful information besides just NAVs.

Figure 6.1 is a snapshot of the website. The fund we're looking at is Central GoldTrust (NYSE: GTU), which is a closed-end fund that holds gold bullion.

Toward the upper right-hand corner, it says the NAV is $64.86 and the market price is $65.94.

That means the value of the assets in the fund is $64.86 per share. However, to buy it, you'd have to pay more than that—$65.94 to be exact.

Two lines below is where you can see how much the premium or discount is for the fund—in this case, Central GoldTrust trades at a premium of 1.67%. In other words, for every $100 in assets, you're paying $101.67. Tomorrow that might change. If there are a bunch of investors who want to sell and no buyers, the sellers will have to lower their asking price to attract buyers, which will reduce the premium. Or the premium could go higher if there are more buyers than sellers, just as with a stock.

But why would an investor in his right mind pay $101.67 for $100 in assets or $65.94 for $64.86 in assets? For the same reason he buys any stock: because he thinks it's going higher. After all, investors pay more for stocks than their book value per share. Investors also pay higher prices or valuations for some stocks compared with their peers with the same book value per share.

> Book value per share: The amount the company would be worth if its business were liquidated. It is calculated by subtracting liabilities from assets and dividend by the number of shares outstanding. An easier way of doing it is dividing shareholders' equity by number of shares outstanding.

Keep in mind, there are two forces at work here—supply and demand as well as the NAV. Theoretically, if the NAV increases, so should the stock price. It doesn't always work that way. If no one is interested in buying the stock, even if the NAV is going higher, the stock price will not follow the NAV. But usually, if the NAV steadily increases, so will the price.

Additionally, supply and demand forces may move the price higher, even if the NAV doesn't. For example, let's say gold goes on a tear again and everyone is piling into gold. Maybe the price of gold goes up 10%, but the price of the closed-end fund rises 15% as the premium increases, reflecting the higher demand. At that point, you may have a fund with an NAV of $71 per share but a stock price of $76 for a premium of 7%.

Discounts and premiums get tightened and widened all the time depending on the market, which sectors are hot, and sentiment. The best scenario is when you buy a fund at a discount, the NAV goes up, and the price eventually closes that discount to trade at a premium.

Let's look at another fund, Deutsche Municipal Income Trust (NYSE: KTF). Even though this is a municipal bond fund, it trades like a stock. On the CEFA website is a chart that shows the fluctuation of the discount or premium for all closed-end funds. It's on the bottom half of the page on the left-hand side and is seen in Figure 6.2.

The light grey line is the important one as that represents the actual discount and premium of the fund. The black line represents the class of funds (in this case municipal bond funds) so that you can compare the fund with its peers.

You can see that the fund started out with about a 1.52% discount and quickly rose to a 3.48% premium. Over the next 10 years, it traded mostly at a discount, hitting a low of a 16.52% discount in late 2008. At that time, you could have bought $100 in assets for less than $84.

The 10-year average discount is 4.917% (the minus sign means discount). The five-year average discount is 5.503%, and year to date, the average discount is 0.38%.

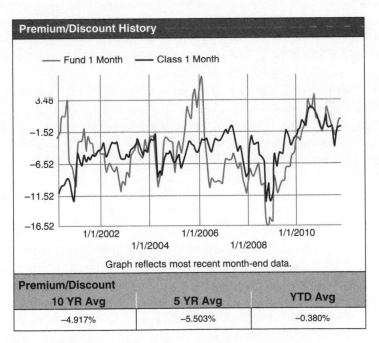

Figure 6.2 Deutsche Municipal Income Trust

Source: Closed-End Fund Association and Lipper, a Thomson Reuters Company

	10 YR	5 YR	1 YR	YTD
Market Return	2.23%	2.18%	4.18%	−2.86%
Lipper Pct. Rank	34	60	67	84
NAV Return	2.99%	2.27%	6.36%	0.61%
Lipper Pct. Rank	25	34	38	38

Figure 6.3 Average Annual Total Return %

Source: Closed-End Fund Association and Lipper, a Thomson Reuters Company

Let's look at one more picture so that you can see how the NAV and the stock price don't always move at the same pace.

We'll zoom in on the CEFA website and look at another closed-end fund. On the top half of the page on the left under the chart, we see a table that looks like the one in Figure 6.3.

The fund is the Liberty All-Star Growth Fund (NYSE: ASG). In each of the periods shown, the NAV outperformed the fund's price (market return is the return of the fund based on its price, not NAV). Over the past year and year to date, the difference has been significant—over 2% in the past one year and more than 3% year to date. In fact, the NAV was actually positive (barely) year to date, while the price of the fund lost 2.86%.

The difference between the returns of the NAV and the price goes back to supply and demand for the fund itself. The fund's price will outperform the NAV as more investors clamor to buy the fund. When that occurs, existing owners raise their price, just as with any stock.

In Liberty All-Star's situation, that was not the case year to date. Although the NAV rose, there were likely more sellers than buyers as the price of the fund fell nearly 3%.

Quite a few closed-end funds pay significant yields. Many of them combine investments, such as common stocks, preferred stocks, and fixed income, to provide a fairly high regular dividend. There are many bond funds to choose from in nearly every category—mortgage-backed securities, corporates, government, foreign government, foreign corporates, business loans, bank loans, and so on. About the only thing missing is a fund that invests in loans made by Jimmy "Knuckles" at the bar on the corner. And rumor has it the First American Loan Shark Interest Trust fund is debuting next year.

Income-paying, closed-end funds can be very attractive because of their high yields. When you have an investment that pays a decent yield, whose stock price trades 10% to 20% below the value of the fund's assets, those yields become even more enticing. But you should check these funds out carefully.

Wall Street is not in the habit of giving away free money. If a fund has a yield of 14% when 10-year Treasuries are paying 2.5% and a strong common stock yield is 4%, you should have a clear understanding of why the fund's yield is so high. Are the assets distressed? Is the dividend sustainable? Will the fund company remain solvent?

For example, some closed-end funds are known as buy-write funds. They invest in stocks, often dividend payers, and then sell calls against those stocks, boosting the yield.

Sounds like a great way to increase the income that the investment produces. And it can be. (We go into further detail in Chapter 10.) The problem can arise when the investments in the funds aren't generating enough income to keep the sky-high dividend sustainable.

Here's what I mean. Let's assume there is $1 million in the fund. The assets in the fund generate $50,000 in income, or 5%. However, the fund has promised investors a 10% yield. That means the fund managers have to dip into the capital to send investors their $100,000 in income. They'll use the $50,000 in income that the investments generated, take $50,000 out of the $1 million, and send the total back to investors.

That's called a return of capital. Return of capital distributions actually can have some tax benefits because they are not taxed like dividends. Return of capital is usually tax deferred and comes off the cost of your investment.

Avoid the Tax Man

For example, you buy a fund for $10 and receive $1 in distributions that are all return of capital (none of it is classified as a dividend). Generally speaking, you will not pay any income tax on the $1 distribution this year. Instead, your cost basis will decrease from $10 to $9. When you eventually sell the stock, you will be taxed as if you'd bought it at $9.

Every time you receive a return of capital distribution, your cost basis will be lowered.

Some of these buy-write funds pay a large distribution that is classified as a return of capital, but it's not quite as I described it, where an investor receives her own money back.

When a company sells an option against a stock and collects the premium, the premium paid out to investors also is considered a return of capital. The option premium is not classified as a capital gain. The fund didn't sell a stock for a gain to generate that cash to pay the dividend. Therefore, the distribution is considered a return of capital, enabling investors to enjoy some tax-deferred income.

Boxing, the Stones, and Taxes

I know about a lot of things. Ask me anything about boxing (Joe Louis was the greatest heavyweight champion), the Rolling Stones ("She's So Cold" is the most underappreciated Stones song), and the stock market (buy low, sell high). One subject I don't profess to be an expert on is taxes. Consult your tax professional with any questions specific to your situation.

One last note about closed-end funds: The specific funds mentioned in this chapter are just for illustrative purposes and are not recommendations.

MLPs

Now that you understand the concept of return of capital, let's examine master limited partnerships (MLPs). An MLP is a company that has a special structure that bypasses corporate taxes because it passes along (nearly) all of its profits to its unitholders in the form of a distribution. A bit of lingo—MLPs have units, not shares, and pay distributions, not dividends. This isn't just jargon; there are important differences from a tax perspective.

These distributions are treated as returns of capital by the Internal Revenue Service (IRS), so investing in MLPs can be a tax-deferred strategy for generating income. As we discussed in the section on closed-end funds, the return of capital lowers your cost basis.

I'm simplifying things with this example, but if you bought an MLP at $25 per share and for 10 years received a $1 per share distribution that was all return of capital, your cost basis would be reduced to $15.

Over those 10 years, you would not pay taxes on those $10 in distributions ($1 × 10 years). However, when you sell, you will pay a capital gain tax on the difference between $15 and the selling price.

If your cost basis eventually goes down to zero, the income you receive will be taxed from that point forward—usually at the capital gains rate.

The distribution most MLPs pay is usually 80% to 90% return of capital. But each MLP is different and the distribution may vary from year to year. Be sure to read the investor relations page of the website of any MLP you are considering investing in to get a thorough understanding of the way the company pays distributions.

Talk to your tax professional before investing in MLPs, because the tax implications can be complex. Additionally, you receive a K-1 tax form from the company, which is different from the 1099-DIV that you get from regular dividend-paying companies. This can add to the cost and timeliness of your tax preparation.

About 80% of MLPs are energy companies. Most of them are oil and gas pipelines that aren't affected much by the price of oil or gas. Their businesses rely on the volume of product that flows through their pipelines.

Other MLPs include infrastructure companies, amusement parks, financial firms, and even a cemetery operator.

MLPs are popular with income investors because of their strong tax-deferred distributions. The risk is that since all of the company's profits are distributed back to shareholders, any decrease in earnings can result in a dividend cut. Although the distribution is high, it is usually not as stable as a strong dividend player, like Clorox, which pays out only 66% of its profits in dividends and has raised its dividend for 37 consecutive years.

However, there are several MLPs that are also Perpetual Dividend Raisers. Plains All American Pipeline (NYSE: PAA) has raised its distribution for 13 consecutive years, and TC Pipelines (NYSE: TCP) has a 15-year streak of annual distribution increases.

The (Very) Final Word on MLPs

MLPs can be an effective tool for estate planning. When an MLP investor passes away, the heirs inherit the stock at the market price at the time of death (similar to a regular stock). So the cost basis, which had been lowered, is adjusted to the price at death. It's like resetting the meter.

The reason it can be effective for estate planning is it may allow the original investor to collect years of tax-deferred income. When he passes, no taxes are collected on that income, and the heirs start all over again.

Here's an example.

An investor buys 10,000 units of an MLP at $25. It pays a 5% distribution yield of $1.25 per unit that is all return of capital. Each year, the unitholder receives $12,500 and does not pay any taxes on the income.

In 10 years, the unitholder has collected $125,000 in tax-deferred income, which has been invested in other assets or used for living expenses.

After eating the fettuccine Alfredo at Marc Lichtenfeld's Authentic Italian Trattoria every day for 10 years, the investor succumbs to a heart attack (it was worth it; the homemade Alfredo sauce is outstanding). The deceased investor's cost basis is now $12.50 because he has received $1.25 for 10 years ($1.25 × 10 = $12.50 and $25 − 12.50 = $12.50).

However, the MLP is now trading at $40. The heirs take over the MLP with a cost basis of $40 and can begin collecting the tax-deferred income for years. Meanwhile, the original investor never paid taxes on the $125,000 in income.

Eat it, IRS!

REITs

Real estate investment trusts (REITs) are also very popular with income investors. A REIT is a company that has a collection of real estate, usually rental properties. Like an MLP, a REIT does not pay corporate taxes and instead must distribute the profits back to shareholders. So REITs often have fairly high yields.

There are REITs for nearly everything: REITs that specialize in apartment buildings, office buildings, shopping centers, hospitals, medical offices, nursing homes, data storage centers. . . .

REITs do not have the same tax implications as MLPs. In an MLP, you are considered a partner in the business. In a REIT, you are a shareholder. The dividends you receive from a REIT will usually be taxed as ordinary income, not at the dividend tax rate, although a portion of the income you receive may be considered return of capital, which would be tax deferred and would lower your cost basis, similar to an MLP. (However, it's usually a much smaller percentage than with an MLP.)

Again—and I can't stress this enough—talk to your tax professional about any questions you may have.

REITs can be volatile, just like the real estate market. If real estate values fall, so do the NAVs of the properties the REIT owns. Additionally, a weak economy can lead to a greater number of vacancies, reducing profits and, as a result, the dividend. A change in interest rates may make borrowing money more difficult for the REIT, lowering its growth rate, or making it tougher for its tenants to pay the rent.

Of course, the opposite is true. During the real estate bubble, the MSCI REIT Index rose 43% between January 2005 and January 2007 (of course, many houses appreciated considerably more), but it plummeted 78% over the next two years as real estate prices collapsed.

Examples of REITs that are also Perpetual Dividend Raisers include Health Care REIT (NYSE: HCN), which owns housing facilities for seniors and other health care–related properties and has lifted its dividend for 11 straight years—and Tanger Factory Outlet Centers (NYSE: SKT), which develops and operates shopping centers and has boosted its dividend every year since 1993.

BDCs

A business development company (BDC) is a publicly traded private equity investment firm. Usually you need boatloads of money or connections to get into a private equity investment. Not too many common folk were able to buy into Facebook before it went public.

Private equity firms create funds and usually invest in early-stage start-up companies. They can be anything from a biotech company with a new technology for treating cancer to a chain of coffeehouses. Some private equity companies specialize in certain sectors, such as biotech, technology, or retail; others are generalists, entertaining opportunities wherever they lie.

Why would someone invest in a private equity fund? We all know how wealthy you could have become if you had invested in Microsoft and Apple when the companies had their initial public offerings

(IPOs). Imagine how rich you would have been if you had invested even before they went public.

When early-stage companies are private and raising money, they can still sell shares, just not to the public in the markets. They sell them in privately arranged transactions. These transactions may be facilitated by pretty much anyone—an investment bank, a board member, or the CEO's mom.

These kinds of deals are usually done by knowing the right people. When looking for funding for Marc Lichtenfeld's Authentic Italian Trattoria, I may have reached out to some well-heeled investors whom I know have funds dedicated to this type of speculation. Or my mom may have mentioned it to her mahjong group, and one of her friends decided to invest $100,000 with me.

When you invest in an early-stage company, you typically get a larger portion of equity than if you bought shares once the company's stock is publicly traded. In 2004, venture capitalist Peter Thiel invested $500,000 in Facebook (NYSE: FB). For his half-a-million-dollar investment he received 10.2% of the company.

When Facebook went public in 2012, a $500,000 investment would have bought just 0.0005% of the company.

Today, a 10.2% stake in Facebook is worth over $21 billion. A 0.005% holding is worth just over $1 million.

Young companies have to sell larger portions of themselves early on to attract investment dollars. Those equity positions can become very lucrative as a company matures and particularly if it goes public.

Sometimes these private equity firms lend money to the start-up (or even more mature companies) instead of taking an equity position. For early-stage companies with little revenue, getting a business loan can be difficult, particularly now that money is tight; for this reason, the start-ups may have to go to other sources.

A private equity firm may lend money to a start-up at, let's say, 13% annual interest, even though the standard bank business loan might be 8%. Since the start-up can't get a bank loan, it has to pony up the higher interest rate since the risk is larger.

Each loan is structured differently, but it is common for the lender to take an equity position or take possession of collateral, such as intellectual property, product, or equipment, if the loan is not paid back.

BDCs that specialize in equity investments may have more inconsistent dividends as their payout could depend on when they are able to sell their positions. If a BDC sells $10 million worth of stock in one quarter and only $2 million in another, depending on the company's dividend policy, the dividend may fluctuate.

However, the BDC that makes a lot of equity investments may have more upside potential or some very strong yields during good years.

BDCs that specialize in making loans to companies may have more reliable dividends as they can pretty much project what their income stream will be from loan payments (assuming the default rate isn't higher than expected). So in that case, you may have less upside but more consistency when it comes to income.

That being said, just because a BDC lends capital to other companies doesn't mean you can't get a high yield.

As I write this, New Mountain Finance (Nasdaq: NMFC) pays a 9.2% yield. New Mountain lends money to cash flow–positive companies, often in a particular niche that has high barriers to entry (difficult for new competitors to enter the space).

Like closed-end funds, BDCs also have an NAV that helps determine the price of the stock but ultimately rely on supply and demand. It's usually best if you can find a high-yielding BDC trading below NAV, though in a low interest rate environment, that's not always easy to do as investors are willing to pay up for more yield.

You Don't Have to Play Mahjong with Mrs. Zuckerberg

Many investors would love the opportunity to get in on the early stages of exciting new companies. But unless you play mahjong with the mother of the next Mark Zuckerberg (founder and CEO of Facebook), or you're otherwise well connected, learning about these opportunities can be difficult.

BDCs allow the everyday investor to get involved with a portfolio of companies, spreading out the risk and very often paying a nice income stream.

For example, Main Street Capital Corporation (Nasdaq: MAIN) is a $1.4 billion market cap BDC that, as of October 2014, paid a yield of about 6.7%.

It makes both equity and debt investments and has a wide variety of companies in its portfolio, including:

- Hydratec Holdings, LLC, a Delano, California, manufacturer of microirrigation systems for farmers
- River Aggregates, LLC, a Porter, Texas, sand and gravel supplier
- Ziegler's New York Pizza Department, a Phoenix, Arizona, pizza chain

Many BDCs pay a robust yield, but as with any investment, there is no such thing as a free lunch. (Unless you're an investor in Main Street—maybe Ziegler's hooks you up with a free slice of pizza. I don't know, but it's worth a shot.) The higher the yield (or potential reward), the higher the risk. So if you're considering investing in a BDC with a high yield, do your homework on the company, see how consistent the dividend has been, and try to ascertain whether it will be sustainable.

Doing that might not be as easy as with your typical dividend-paying company, where you can look and see how many widgets it sells and what its profit margins and cash flow are. However, if a BDC has a long and consistent track record, you should have a bit more confidence that it can continue paying the dividend.

As with a REIT, the IRS treats a BDC's dividend differently. To pay no corporate income tax, a BDC must pass through at least 90% of its profits on to shareholders. Most pass an even higher percentage of the profits on.

Generally, you'll be taxed on the kind of income the BDC received. If it earns interest on a loan, you probably will be taxed on that portion as ordinary income. If it sells a company for a capital gain, you will be taxed on that portion at the capital gain rate.

The BDC will send you a form with the breakdown, so you'll have all the information you'll need.

Once again, if you have any tax-related questions, repeat this with me now: Talk to your tax professional.

Closed-end funds, MLPs, REITs, and BDCs can be an excellent way to add yield to your income portfolio. Many of these businesses generate a ton of cash and must pass that cash along to shareholders, which is why they are able to pay investors more than other companies can.

When ExxonMobil makes a profit, management decides what do to with that cash. Does it invest in new equipment, put a gym in the corporate headquarters, buy back stock, or give some back to shareholders in the form of a dividend? MLPs, REITs, and BDCs, by the laws of their corporate structure, *must* return profits to shareholders.

Keep in mind that such investments can be volatile as they are usually concentrated in one (often-cyclical) sector and have more complex tax ramifications for shareholders. But if you don't mind doing a little homework and talking to your tax professional (or handling it yourself with tax software), these investments can be an excellent way to boost the amount of income you receive every year.

Preferred Stocks

Preferred stocks are sort of a combination of a bond and a stock. They pay a higher dividend, sometimes can be converted into common stock, and are higher in the pecking order than common stock if the company is liquidated. However, they come after bonds in that situation.

If a company declares bankruptcy and its assets are sold off, bondholders will be paid first. Next come preferred shareholders, then shareholders of common stock.

Many preferred shares, known as cumulative preferred stock, will accumulate if the dividend is not paid. When a dividend of a common stock is not paid or is cut, the shareholder is out of luck. If, sometime in the future, the company reestablishes a dividend, the shareholder starts from whatever dividend the company declared.

Cumulative preferred shareholders, however, see their dividends accumulate during the period that the company did not pay dividends. So if a company has an annual preferred dividend of $1 per share, stops paying a dividend for two years, and later introduces a $1 preferred dividend in year 3, the preferred shareholders will have to get paid out $3 per share ($1 plus the $2 missed) before any common shareholders can receive a dividend.

Because of this greater stability, preferred shares are not as volatile as common stock. Preferred share investors typically will not see the swings in share price that investors will see with common shares—although during the financial crisis of 2008 and 2009, numerous preferred shares of financial stocks were decimated because of fears that the companies might collapse. However, many of them came roaring back in 2009 and 2010.

Because preferreds have high yields, they often behave similarly to bonds in that interest rates affect the prices. Just like a bond, rising interest rates will likely lower the price of a preferred stock.

Also like a bond, a preferred is issued at par value, and the dividend is usually fixed. The dividend is not going to grow like a Perpetual Dividend Raiser. But for some investors, particularly those who need the income now, the higher rate today may be worth sacrificing growth tomorrow.

Another similarity to bonds—the dividend is rated by credit rating agencies. And unlike a stock, preferred shareholders have no voting rights. They are not owners of the company; they are creditors.

Financial institutions make up about 85% of all preferreds, so if the financial sector is strong, preferreds should do well. If financials are weak, as they were during the 2008 crisis, preferreds will be hit hard.

For example, insurer MetLife has the MetLife preferred stock, Series B (NYSE: METPrB), that pays a fixed rate of 6.5% annually (on the par value, which is $25), with dividends paid quarterly. As I write this, it is trading at $25.41, slightly above par value, so the yield is 6.4%. If you can buy a stock below par, you can get a yield higher than the declared yield, just like a bond.

> Par value: The face value (price at which it was first offered) of a bond or preferred stock.

Preferred stocks are often redeemable 30 years after they are issued, although some have no redemption date. Of course, you can always sell the stocks in the open market; however, they are generally not as liquid as common stock.

I'm not a huge fan of preferreds because they are much closer to bonds than to stocks and typically don't grow dividends. A 6.5% yield might be attractive today, but it won't keep up with inflation, even a low level of inflation, such as 3%.

Think about it this way. If you invest $1,000 in a preferred with a 6.5% yield, you'll receive $65 per year. However, in three years at 3% inflation, you'll need $1,092 to have the same buying power as $1,000 three years prior. Your $65 per year won't keep up with inflation. You need a dividend growing faster than inflation to do that.

The benefit of a preferred stock is that the dividend is higher than a stock, particularly for a blue chip company. The downside is that it probably will not keep pace with inflation. Also, most preferreds do not let you reinvest the dividends in more preferred shares. Some let you reinvest the preferred dividends into common stock, however.

Like some of the other higher-yielding, less traditional income investments, there's nothing wrong with sprinkling one or two preferreds into a portfolio. But since preferreds are a kind of quasibond, you want the majority of your holdings to be Perpetual Dividend Raisers.

Summary

- Closed-end funds are mutual funds that trade like stocks.
- Return of capital is a cash distribution that is tax deferred and lowers your cost basis.
- REITs invest in real estate assets.
- MLPs are partnerships, often energy pipelines.
- BDCs are similar to publicly traded private equity firms.
- Preferred stocks are as much like bonds as they are like stocks.
- Closed-end funds, REITs, MLPs, BDCs, and preferred stocks are alternatives to regular dividend payers in that they usually have higher-than-average yields—but they can have complex tax implications as well.
- Playing mahjong with Mrs. Zuckerberg might be a great way to get lucrative investing ideas.

What You Need to Know to Set Up a Portfolio

You've heard the well-worn saying "Don't put all your eggs in one basket." That's why most financial professionals recommend you diversify your investments across a variety of assets.

Normally, you don't want to be 100% in stocks or 100% in bonds. You want a good mix of assets so that if one asset class is underperforming, there's a good chance another one is outperforming.

Typically, you want to own a mixture of stocks, bonds, real estate, precious metals, and maybe some commodities or other investments. The recent financial crisis is a good example of how this type of portfolio can balance things out.

While stocks and housing were crashing in 2008 and early 2009, bonds, gold, and commodities performed well. An investor who was well diversified lost less than one who was primarily in stocks and real estate. I knew plenty of people who lost everything because all of their money was tied up in real estate—the very same people who told me just two years earlier that "Real estate is the only way to make money."

Next time someone tells you that one specific way is the "only way to make money," figure out a way to short that person's net worth, because it's heading south within a few years. I guarantee it. I don't care if the way is gold, real estate, stocks, or Italian trattorias. When people are so arrogant about their investments (even if they're usually smart investors) that they've concluded it's infeasible for there to be a better way to make money, that means that investment is likely at a top and heading lower.

Within any asset class, it makes sense to diversify as well.

If you own a portfolio of rental properties, you wouldn't want to own houses that were all on the same block. If that block suddenly becomes undesirable, your portfolio will take a big hit.

You'd want to have houses spread out all over town or maybe even all over the country. If your house in Florida takes a big hit in price, perhaps the apartment in California will hold its value. If rental prices slide in New Jersey, maybe they're going up in Colorado.

It's the same with stocks and mutual funds. In fact, the Oxford Club, where I am the Chief Income Strategist, has an asset allocation model consisting of stocks, bonds, precious metals, and real estate.

Within the stocks asset class, we further sort (and diversify) them into large caps, small caps, international (further categorized into Pacific Rim and European), real estate investment trusts (REITs), and so on.

Bonds are diversified as well. Our bond recommendations include short-term corporates, high-yield corporates, and Treasury Inflation-Protected Securities (TIPS).

A portfolio of dividend stocks should be the same. Although it may be tempting to load up on dividend payers with 10% yields, that's likely a recipe for disaster. There's nothing wrong with sprinkling a few of those into a well-diversified portfolio to boost yield, but if all you are holding are stocks with double-digit yields, you are taking on way too much risk.

Generally speaking, you want to diversify your dividend-paying stocks across different yields and sectors.

You'll want industrials, technology, energy (often master limited partnerships [MLPs]), REITS, health care, consumer staples, and a host of other sectors.

You'll constantly have some group in the market outperforming and another underperforming. So by diversifying, you are trying to ensure you always have exposure to a group that is performing well.

If consumer stocks are weak, perhaps health care will remain strong. When the economy is starting to show signs of recovery, industrials should work.

There will always be a group on the rise, either because of the cyclical nature of stocks and the economy or because a certain sector gets hot.

If Warren Buffett suddenly announces that he is buying large pharmaceutical companies, you'll want to have already bought into that sector because they are likely going to take off for a few weeks or months. Deciding to get in once Warren Buffett proclaims that he likes those stocks on CNBC will be too late. The market will have already reacted, and the price of those stocks will be significantly higher half a second after the Oracle utters those words.

But if you have a diversified portfolio, where you already own some large pharmaceutical stocks, when Buffett says he likes big pharma, your shares of Bristol-Myers Squibb (NYSE: BMY) and Abbott Laboratories, which you bought two years ago, 15% lower, will take off.

And important for dividend investors, your yield will remain the same. It doesn't matter what the stock price is today; it matters what you paid for it.

That's an important difference for the investor who either needs the income today or is trying to build a wealth-creating portfolio for the long term.

The *Oxford Income Letter* Portfolio—An Example

I manage the three portfolios for the Oxford Club's *Oxford Income Letter*. The Instant Income Portfolio uses my 10–11–12 System to generate a high level of income today and even more tomorrow. The Compound Income Portfolio also uses my 10–11–12 System and is for investors who don't need the income today and instead want to use the power of compounding to grow their wealth by reinvesting the dividends. The third portfolio is the Retirement Catch-Up/ High Yield Portfolio, which docs not use my 10–11–12 System and is for investors who can handle a higher degree of risk in exchange for higher yield.

I'm not going to mention what stocks are in the portfolios because by the time you read this, the portfolios may very well have changed. For more information on the portfolios, please visit www.oxfordincomeletter.com or www.oxfordclub.com.

However, I will tell you how the portfolios are currently diversified. Again, this may change by the time you read this, so don't take this as gospel. But as you'll see, it's a good mix of stocks that should let us participate in strong markets and keep us from getting badly hurt if any one sector or stock blows up.

As of September 2014, the Instant Income Portfolio consisted of eight positions. The stocks are in these sectors:

Consumer:	2
Defense:	1
Energy:	1
REITs:	2
Technology:	1
Telecom:	1

The Compound Income Portfolio has 15 stocks from the following sectors:

Agriculture:	1
Consumer:	4
Defense:	1
Energy:	2
REITs:	3 (1 healthcare related)
Technology:	1
Telecom:	2
Waste management:	1

And the Retirement Catch-Up/High Yield Portfolio has eight stocks in these sectors:

Business development companies (BDCs):	2
Broadcasting:	1
Energy:	3
Health care:	1
Preferred stock:	1

Source: The Oxford Club, the *Oxford Income Letter*, September 2014

We have a diversity of yields as well. As I mentioned, we can't just load up on stocks paying 10% dividends, for reasons I'll explain later in this chapter. Although we want the yield as high as possible, we need to take into account risk and the growth of the dividend.

I would rather own a stock paying a 4% yield that grows its dividend every year by 10% than one with a 6% yield and a dividend growth of 3%.

If I'm holding these stocks for the long term, a stock with a current 4% yield but 10% growth will yield more than the 6% stock with 3% growth in seven and a half years.

By year 10, the stock that started out with the lower dividend payment will yield 9.4%; the one that started out higher will deliver only 7.8%.

So, for long-term holders, dividend growth is just as, if not more, important than current yield.

The *Oxford Income Letter* portfolios' stocks have these yields (based on the price when they entered the portfolio)

The Instant Income Portfolio	
7.3%	
4.3%	
4.2%	
3.8%	
5.2%	
6.4%	
5.8%	
3.6%	
Average	5.1%

The Compound Income Portfolio	
4.6%	
4.2%	
3.5%	
6.8%	
3.6%	
5.2%	
6.8%	
4.5%	
5.2%	
6.5%	
5.5%	
4.1%	
5.8%	
3.8%	
4.9%	
Average	5.0%

The Retirement Catch-Up/High Yield Portfolio	
7.3%	
6.8%	
10.0%	
9.7%	
10.3%	
4.6%	
7.7%	
9.6%	
6.0%	
Average	8.0%

Source: Oxford Club, the *Oxford Income Letter*

You can see we've got a few stocks with high yields in there: In the Instant Income Portfolio we have one that yields 7.3%. In the Compound Income Portfolio we have two stocks that yield 6.8%. These high-dividend payers help us get the average yield over 5%, which is very healthy in today's market. But we also have some lower-yielding stocks, such as a defense contractor that yields 3.6%, an insurance company that yields 3.1%, and a technology company that yields 3.5%.

If something should happen to our 7.3% stock and the company has to cut the dividend, the share price will slide considerably. However, our 3.6% defense contractor and 3.5% technology company should stand up over the years, as they have for decades.

Now that I've established the importance of diversification, let's go ahead and talk about how to pick dividend-paying stocks.

Setting Up the Portfolio

The first thing you need to do is answer these questions:

1. What is your time frame?
2. What is the purpose of the portfolio: income or wealth creation?

If the answer to question 1 is three years or less, put down this book, and look at something less risky than stocks. Really, the only thing you should be looking at are money market accounts, certificates of deposit, Treasuries, and maybe very highly rated corporates that mature in three years.

If you need the money back in three years, you shouldn't be taking much risk with it. Of course, the bonds that are available will pay you practically nothing in today's interest rate environment, but at least you'll be sure that your money will be there when you need it.

Even blue chip stocks with 50-year track records of raising the dividend will fall in a bear market.

One of my favorite Perpetual Dividend Raisers, Genuine Parts, which has been hiking its dividend every year since 1956, saw its stock price cut in half from its peak in 2007 to the lows of 2008.

Granted, the financial collapse of 2008 and early 2009 was a rare event, but for anyone who needed his or her capital back in 2008, the reason the market fell or the uniqueness of the selloff didn't matter. The fact was, investors' money was not available when they needed it. It was gone.

By the way, patient investors who were able to ride out the storm of 2008 (and, I hope, reinvest those dividends at low prices) saw Genuine Parts' stock come roaring back, more than doubling in two years. As of September 2014, it was trading 70% higher than its high in 2007, before it started to slide. Shareholders who reinvested their dividends in March 2009 were able to buy shares as low as $27.05. The stock hit $90 in early 2014.

In fact, the 2008 collapse taught many investors a valuable lesson—to hang on despite a nasty bear market. Even investors who bought at the very top in 2007 and survived a 57% haircut were made whole five years later and had significant gains within seven years.

But if you need your funds now or in the near future, to live on in retirement, to pay for school, or for a host of other reasons that mean the money can't be at risk, stocks, even stable dividend stocks, are not the answer.

However, if your time horizon is at least five years, this portfolio should work out great.

Ultimately, this portfolio works best with a 10-year or longer time. The compounding nature of the rising dividends really kicks into gear starting around year 8 or 9. The longer you can go without touching the principal, the better.

If you can go beyond 10 years, that's where significant wealth starts to get created.

If you buy a stock with a 4.5% dividend yield and the company raises its dividend by 10% each year, in 10 years, your stock will be yielding 10.6%.

Assuming a straight dividend payout (no dividend reinvestment), after 10 years you'll have collected 71% of your principal back in dividends.

But watch what happens because of the power of compounding as the years go on.

After 12.5 years, your investment will have been fully paid for by the dividends you've collected, and you'll be earning a 13% yield.

In year 15, the yield on your original investment will be 17%.

In year 18, you'll have collected dividends equal to double your original investment. Notice how it took 12.5 years to capture 100% of your capital back in dividends and fewer than six years to do it again. Compounding is a powerful tool.

At the end of year 20, you'll be earning 27% yield every year and will have earned dividends equal to 250% of your original investment.

Keep in mind that the yield I just discussed has nothing to do with the stock price. The stock could have tripled during this time, or it could have been cut in half. As long as the company is paying and raising its dividend by 10% per year, those are the yields you would have enjoyed.

The numbers get even more astounding when you reinvest those dividends, as I'll show you in the next chapter.

Remember that most companies do not raise their dividend by the same percentage every year. But some companies do have a target range for their dividend growth rate. And a number of companies have averaged 10% per year dividend hikes over 10 years. It might not have been 10% every year. One year might have been 5%; the next, 15%. But over the course of the 10 years, the average was 10%.

In a perfect world, we're going to have Warren Buffett's desired holding period, which is for life. If we can hang on to these investments forever, they should continue to generate increasing amounts of income for us every year.

Of course, not everyone has Buffett's flexibility. Many investors need to eventually sell stock to fund their retirement. But if you can put off selling for as long as possible, it will help ensure the additional income is there when you need it.

Last, whether you need the income today or you're trying to create wealth for tomorrow will determine what you do with the dividends.

Those who need income today will collect the dividends when they are paid, usually every quarter. Investors who rely on dividends for income typically keep track of when their dividends will arrive.

Some investors, particularly retirees, may be tempted to factor when the dividends will arrive in their decision as to which stocks they're going to buy. They like the idea of checks coming in regularly every week or so. With a portfolio of 10 to 20 stocks, you probably could structure it so that you are receiving dividends as regularly as you wish.

Companies that pay monthly dividends rather than quarterly are particularly popular with those on a fixed income.

However, I wouldn't invest that way. Deciding which stocks you're going to buy based on which week of the quarter they happen to pay out their dividend is not a smart thing to do.

You want to pick the very best stocks that offer the juiciest yield with the greatest degree of safety and opportunity for dividend growth. These three factors should be your main criteria.

The company isn't taking your schedule into account. It could delay the dividend by a week or two in a certain quarter, which could mean you don't receive the dividend when you are counting on it.

If you focus on exactly when you will receive a dividend check, you'll limit yourself and possibly miss the best opportunities in the market at that time.

If you're only looking for a stock with a dividend payout in January, April, August, and October, for example, you might not invest in one with a safer dividend, a higher yield, and better growth opportunities.

Of course, once you own the stocks, you can set up your calendar so that you know when the dividends are expected to arrive, but don't buy the stocks according to when the payouts are due.

Don't Try to Time Your Dividend Payments

Don't buy dividend stocks based on when the dividends are expected. Instead, buy the very best stocks you can find. Don't let the calendar limit you.

Yields

If you need the income now, do *not* figure out how much dividend income you need and pick the stocks that will deliver. That's a recipe for disaster. You're too likely to cut corners and choose stocks that may not meet your otherwise stringent criteria. You may focus only on how much money you'll get today and not enough on growth and safety.

Instead, find the very best stocks, and see whether they meet your income goals. If they don't meet your objectives, go through your proposed portfolio, and see which stocks you can substitute without sacrificing safety or growth.

> Yield: The percentage of interest or dividends an investor receives, based on the cost of the investment. To calculate yield, divide the amount of the dividend by the price of the stock.
>
> Example: A stock is trading at $20 and pays a dividend of $1 per share. $1 divided by $20 equals 0.05, or 5%.
>
> Note that an investor's yield does not change if the price of the stock changes. If in the example, the investor bought the stock at $20 and it went up to $25, the yield would still be 5%, as he will receive $1 per share for each $20 share that he bought. A new investor will have a yield of 4%, as she had to pay $25 per share. The only way an investor's yield changes is if he or she buys more stock at a different price or if the amount of the dividend changes.

Perhaps you'll be able to replace a stock with a 4% yield with another that has a 4.7% yield with only a slightly higher payout ratio and similar growth.

But saying, "I need to earn 7%" and looking only for stocks that can generate 7% yields is going to be a catastrophe. Why? You take on too much risk to obtain those higher yields.

You know the expression "There's no such thing as a free lunch." That applies especially to Wall Street. If a stock is paying a yield way above average, there is usually a good reason for it. The reason might be that management believes it must pay a high yield to attract investors. You don't want to buy a stock where management dangles that yield in front of investors like a carrot on a stick. Especially if that yield is not sustainable.

Rather, you want a company with management that pays out a respectable dividend because it believes it should return some shareholders' cash every quarter and it has the funds to do so.

In September 2014, the S&P 500's dividend yield was 1.86%. Over the past 50 years, the average yield has been 1.98%.[1] Generally speaking, I look for companies whose yield is at least one and a half times that of the current S&P 500's and preferably at least two times.

Again, growth and safety of the dividend are more important than the yield, so I may opt for a yield of 3.7% rather than 4.5% if I think it will make for a better investment over the next 10 years.

You also want to be sure your yield will keep up with expected inflation.

Currently, inflation is very low, about 2%. To ensure that your buying power will remain the same or grow in the future, your yield should be above the rate of inflation.

No one knows where inflation will be in five or 10 years, but we can look at historical averages as a guide. Since 1914, inflation has averaged about 3.4% per year, so ideally, you'd like to start your search with a stock paying a 4% yield or more—even higher if it's in a taxable account. (More on taxes in Chapter 12.)

REITs and MLPs often pay significantly higher yields because of their corporate structure, as I explained in Chapter 6. But for now, keep in mind that while they may have a place in your portfolio, you should avoid the temptation of adding too many REITs and MLPs just because of their attractive yields. As we discussed earlier, you want to diversify your portfolio and not get too heavy into any one or two sectors.

In the current environment, I would almost automatically reject anything with a double-digit yield. I say *almost* because there can be a situation where a good stock gets beaten up because of its sector (a baby being thrown out with the bathwater), or perhaps it deserved to get a thrashing but said thrashing was a bit overdone.

But for the most part, a stock yielding 10% should be a warning sign rather than a come-hither sign. If you're going to invest in a stock with that kind of yield, be sure to look at it very carefully.

The first thing you should look at is . . .

View: **Annual Data** | Quarterly Data   All numbers in thousands

Period Ending	Jun 30, 2014	Jun 30, 2013	Jun 30, 2012
Net Income	113,541	123,650	104,372
Operating Activities, Cash Flows Provided By or Used In			
Depreciation	57,511	55,010	56,195
Adjustments To Net Income	27,962	35,392	53,430
Changes In Accounts Receivables	(2,430)	(16,575)	10,197
Changes In Liabilities	(29,336)	38,872	(8,438)
Changes In Inventories	4,133	(5,814)	1,101
Depreciation			
Changes In Other Operating Activities	6,709	(41,448)	(34,927)
Total Cash Flow From Operating Activities	**178,090**	**189,087**	**181,930**
Investing Activities, Cash Flows Provided By or Used In			
Capital Expenditures	(24,822)	(25,969)	(35,718)
Investments	-	-	-
Other Cash flows from Investing Activities	(417,461)	(50,190)	(248,964)
Total Cash Flow From Investing Activities	**(442,283)**	**(76,159)**	**(284,682)**
Financing Activities, Cash Flows Provided By or Used In			
Dividends Paid	(75,392)	(70,527)	(62,994)
Sale Purchase of Stock	(19,341)	(15,215)	(20,973)
Net Borrowings	365,000	(30,000)	185,000
Other Cash Flows from Financing Activities	(2,016)	(770)	(677)
Total Cash Flow From Financing Activities	**273,106**	**(111,074)**	**100,851**
Effect Of Exchange Rate Changes	-	-	-
Change in Cash and Cash Equivalents	**8,913**	**1,854**	**(1,901)**

Figure 7.1   Statement of Cash Flow, Meredith Corp.
Source: Yahoo! Finance

Payout Ratio

The payout ratio is the ratio of the dividends paid versus net income. For example, if a company makes $100 million in profit and pays out $30 million in dividends, its payout ratio is 30%.

> Payout ratio = Dividends paid/Net income

Notice that the payout ratio has nothing to do with yield or dividends per share. We can figure out the payout ratio by looking at the financial statements—the statement of cash flow, to be exact.

Figure 7.1 is the statement of cash flows for Meredith Corp. (NYSE: MDP). Meredith is the publisher of magazines, such as *Ladies' Home Journal, Parents,* and *Family Circle.*

You can see that in the fiscal year ending June 30, 2014, Meredith Corp. paid out $75,392,000 in dividends against $113,541,000 in net income, for a payout ratio of 66%.

The year before, the company paid $70,527,000 in dividends versus $123,650,000 in net income, or a payout ratio of 57%. So the dividend went up, but so did the payout ratio. If net income were much higher, let's say $150,000,000, then the payout ratio would have declined to 50%. So you can (and often do) have a situation where the dividend payment increases, but because net income climbed even more, the payout ratio goes down.

The payout ratio tells you whether the company has enough profits to maintain (or grow) the dividend. If a company has a payout ratio of 66%, as Meredith Corp. did, that means it is paying shareholders $0.66 in dividends of every $1 in profit.

That's a sustainable number and one that has room to grow. If you're considering this company and know that earnings are expected to rise, you could make the assumption that dividends should increase as well, since the payout ratio is only 66%. Considering that Meredith has raised its dividend every year for the past 21 years, it's a safe assumption that as net income climbs, so should the dividend.

The lower the payout ratio, the more room there is to grow the dividend.

If a company's payout ratio is 90%, any decrease in earnings may cause a dividend cut as the company will not be able to afford to pay the full dividend, unless it dips into its capital, which sometimes occurs.

Occasionally you will see companies with payout ratios of over 100%, meaning all of their earnings and some of their cash on hand is going toward the dividend.

That is not sustainable for the long term, and you should avoid investing in those companies.

Often that is the scenario when you see a stock with a yield above 10%. The company is pouring every dollar it can into the dividend to attract investors, but likely it will not be able to continue on that track for too long.

Going back to our example with Meredith Corp., back in 2009, the company paid out $39,730,000 even though it *lost* $107,084,000 during the year.

You may be asking, How could the company pay nearly $40 million in dividends when it lost boatloads of money?

And that would be a very good question.

The answer is because Meredith Corp. was still cash flow positive.

Cash flow: The amount of net cash the company brought in during a specific period.

There is a very big difference between earnings and cash flow. Regulators allow all kinds of noncash deductions that can lower a company's profits.

For example, when a company buys a piece of machinery, it takes depreciation off its profits. However, that depreciation does not affect the cash that the company's operations generated.

Let's create a very simplified income statement to illustrate what I mean, using my Authentic Italian Trattoria. (See Table 7.1.)

Let's assume because of my incredible baked ziti recipe (it really is very good), the restaurant brought in $1 million in revenue. Our cost of goods sold was $500,000, giving us a gross profit of $500,000.

We paid out $300,000 in operating expenses, leaving us with a $200,000 operating profit.

When we opened, we bought a bunch of equipment that depreciates every year. We're allowed to take that depreciation as an expense, which lowers our profit.

Finally, we pay no taxes—not because we have a creative accountant, but because we have losses that we carried forward.

As you can see from the table, the depreciation lowered our net income to $100,000 from what would have been $200,000. But did we really make $100,000, or did we make $200,000?

If we create a statement of cash flow, we add back in all noncash items, like depreciation. Remember, depreciation doesn't represent

Table 7.1   Marc Lichtenfeld's Authentic Italian Trattoria 2014 Income Statement

Revenue	$1,000,000
Cost of goods sold	$500,000
Gross profit	$500,000
Operating expenses	$300,000
Operating profit	$200,000
Depreciation	$100,000
Taxes	$0
Net profit	$100,000

any actual cash that was laid out this year. We paid for the equipment in previous years but now claim depreciation as an expense against our operating profit.

> Depreciation: An accounting method that lets a business expense the cost of equipment over its useful life.
>
> Example: The trattoria buys $1 million worth of equipment and pays for it in the first year. If the equipment should last 10 years, we can take $100,000 as an expense off our profits every year for 10 years, even though we paid the $1 million in the first year.

Let's create a very simplified statement of cash flow where we add back in the depreciation. (See Table 7.2.)

For simplicity's sake, I didn't include other variables that can alter cash flow, so let's just assume that the cash flow from operating activities is the total cash flow from the business.

You can see that while the net income that will be reported to the government for tax purposes is $100,000, the cash flow—the amount of cash the business actually generated—is $200,000.

Going back to our real-life example with Meredith Corp., while it was unprofitable in 2009, it was able to pay the $39,730,000 in dividends because its cash flow from operating activities was $180,920,000.

Even though the company lost over $107 million during the year, its business generated $181 million in cash, which enabled it to pay the dividend.

Calculating the payout ratio based on the cash flow from operations gives us a ratio of just 22%.

Table 7.2   Marc Lichtenfeld's Authentic Italian Trattoria 2014 Statement of Cash Flows

Net Profit	$100,000
Depreciation	$100,000
Total cash flow from operating activities	$200,000

When I look at the payout ratio, I calculate it using free cash flow or cash flow from operations. It's a more accurate representation of whether a company will be able to pay its dividend than using earnings.

Because of the myriad accounting rules, earnings can be (and often are) manipulated to tell the story that management wants to tell.

CEOs are frequently paid bonuses and stock options based on earnings. Stocks tend to follow earnings, so if the CEO has a lot of stock or options, it's in his or her interest to make sure the stock price is high. One surefire way to increase your stock price is to grow your earnings at a rapid clip.

So, CEOs often have a direct financial incentive to make their earnings as high as possible, whether they reflect the truth or not.

Cash flow is a bit harder to fudge. Of course, a motivated executive who wants to commit outright fraud probably can do so, but manipulating cash flow numbers is more difficult as it represents the actual amount of cash the company generated.

Think of it as all of the cash coming in the door minus all of the cash that went out.

Net income is something accountants dreamed up. Cash flow is something businesspeople rely on.

As I mentioned, since stock prices follow earnings over the long haul, you, of course, want to be invested in a company with earnings growth. But for the purpose of analyzing the dividend and its likelihood of being cut or growing in the future, cash flow is a more reliable indicator.

A company can't pay dividends with earnings. It has to pay it with cash.

For that reason, I prefer to use cash flow when determining the payout ratio. Similar to earnings, I generally want to see a payout ratio of 75% or less; if it's a utility, BDC, REIT, or MLP, the payout ratio can be higher.

A payout ratio of less than 75% gives me the confidence that management can continue not only to pay the dividend but also to increase it, even if the business slumps.

A company with a 50% payout ratio (based on cash flow) and a 20-year history of raising dividends, for example, should have no problem raising the dividend next year, even if cash flow slips 10%.

Remember, companies with long histories of raising dividends want to continue to raise them, even if it's just by a penny, to keep their record intact. Management knows that investors are watching closely and that any change in policy will be perceived as a change in outlook.

Dividend Growth Rate

At this point, I'm assuming that any stock you're looking at is one that raises its dividend every year. But a company that inches the dividend half a penny higher each year, simply to make the list of companies that raise dividends, isn't one that will likely help you achieve your goals.

What you need to look at is the dividend growth rate.

There are two ways of doing this. The first way is to go to the DRiP Resource Center (http://dripinvesting.org), which publishes a list of all the stocks with a minimum of five consecutive annual dividend raises.

The Excel spreadsheet that is published every month and is available for you to download for free contains a group of columns headed *DGR*, which stands for dividend growth rate. The spreadsheet shows the percentage growth over the past 1, 3, 5, and 10 years.

Take a look at the spreadsheet in Figure 7.2. You can see that Becton, Dickinson and Company (NYSE: BDX) raised its dividend by 10% in the last year. Over the past three years, the average annual increase was 11.1%. Over five, it was 12.2% and over 10, 17.6%.

That's a very strong record of raises. Unfortunately, at this time, the stock yields only 1.9%, which is why the company may be able to raise the dividend so much each year.

Contrast that with Black Hills Corp. (NYSE: BKH), which raised its dividend only 2.7% last year, 1.8% over 3 years, 1.7% over 5 years, and 2.4% over 10 years.

Ultimately, you want to find a company with a yield you can live with today but that also has a record of meaningful dividend raises so that it will get you to your goals over the years.

There's another column here that may be useful: the column with the header *5/10*. This is the ratio of the average annual dividend raise over five years versus 10 years. This shows whether a company has been raising the dividend more over the past five years than it has on average over 10.

U.S. Dividend Champions (and American Depository Receipts) 25 or more Straight Years Higher Dividends		Dividends Paid by Year (excluding Special/Extra Dividends) *A/D=Acceleration/Deceleration (5-year average) (DGR=Dividend Growth Rate)			
Company Name	Ticker Symbol	5/10 A/D*	DGR 1-yr	DGR 3-yr	DGR 5-yr	DGR 10-yr
1st Source Corp.	SRCE	0.443	3.0	3.7	3.2	7.3
3M Company	MMM	0.724	7.6	6.5	4.9	6.8
ABM Industries Inc.	ABM	0.795	3.4	3.6	3.7	4.7
AFLAC Inc.	AFL	0.484	6.0	7.6	8.1	16.8
Air Products & Chem.	APD	0.844	10.8	13.0	10.3	12.2
Altria Group Inc.	MO	0.810	7.8	8.2	9.2	11.4
American States Water	AWR	1.555	19.7	13.5	8.7	5.6
Archer Daniels Midland	ADM	0.645	8.6	8.2	7.9	12.2
AT&T Inc.	T	0.488	2.3	2.3	2.4	4.9
Atmos Energy	ATO	0.029	2.5	1.8	1.7	1.7
Automatic Data Proc.	ADP	0.615	10.1	8.6	8.4	13.7
Becton Dickinson & Co.	BDX	0.694	10.0	11.1	12.2	17.6
Bemis Company	BMS	0.532	4.0	4.2	3.4	6.4
Black Hills Corp.	BKH	0.693	2.7	1.8	1.7	2.4
Bowl America Class A	BWL_A	0.615	2.3	2.1	1.9	3.1
Brady Corp.	BRC	0.654	2.7	2.8	4.3	6.6
Brown-Forman Class B	BF-B	0.764	10.5	9.7	7.8	10.2
C.R. Bard Inc.	BCR	0.930	5.1	5.4	5.8	6.2
California Water Service	CWT	1.396	1.6	2.5	1.8	1.3
Carlisle Companies	CSL	1.023	10.5	8.4	7.0	6.8
Chevron Corp.	CVX	0.857	11.1	11.2	9.0	10.6
Chubb Corp.	CB	0.672	6.8	5.8	6.2	9.2
Cincinnati Financial	CINF	0.233	1.7	1.2	1.5	6.4
Cintas Corp.	CTAS	0.982	20.3	17.1	10.9	11.0
Clarcor Inc.	CLC	1.327	16.2	13.1	11.7	8.9
Clorox Company	CLX	0.885	8.9	8.7	9.4	10.7
Coca-Cola Company	KO	0.823	9.8	8.4	8.1	9.8
Colgate-Palmolive Co.	CL	0.984	9.0	9.4	11.3	11.4
Commerce Bancshares	CBSH	0.543	6.5	5.2	3.8	7.0
Community Trust Bancorp.	CTBI	0.295	1.6	1.5	1.7	5.9
Computer Services Inc.	CSVI	0.748	13.2	13.5	12.7	17.0
Connecticut Water Service	CTWS	1.253	2.1	1.9	2.2	1.7
Consolidated Edison	ED	1.068	1.7	1.1	1.0	0.9
Diebold Inc.	DBD	0.525	0.9	2.1	2.8	5.4
Donaldson Company	DCI	0.956	42.9	26.4	17.6	18.4
Dover Corp.	DOV	1.023	9.0	10.7	10.0	9.8
Eagle Financial Services	EFSI	0.349	4.1	3.3	2.6	7.3
Eaton Vance Corp.	EV	0.414	5.1	7.5	6.3	15.2
Emerson Electric	EMR	0.801	3.1	7.1	6.2	7.7
Energen Corp.	EGN	0.814	3.6	3.7	3.9	4.7

Figure 7.2 U.S. Dividend Champions

Source: DRiP Resource Center

Think of it as a momentum indicator for dividend raises.

So, in Becton, Dickinson's case, if you divide the 5-year average of 12.7 by the 10-year average of 17.6, you get 0.694. Anything over 1 signifies a 5-year average higher than the 10-year average. Below 1 and the 5-year average is below the 10-year—perhaps signifying that the dividend increases are slowing down.

CLARCOR Inc. (NYSE: CLC), in contrast, has a ratio of 1.327, which tells us that the momentum of the dividend raise has increased in the past five years. And by looking at the one- and three-year figures, we see the increases are continuing to get larger.

I don't have a hard-and-fast rule about this ratio. I'm willing to accept a slower growth rate if it's still meaningful. For example, Colgate-Palmolive raised its dividend by 11.3% annually over the past 5 years and 11.4% over the past 10. But when you look at the one-year growth rate, you can see it slowed to 9.0% over the past year. That's a raise I can live with, because 9% will still outpace the rate of inflation (at least today). Considering after the Great Recession, the economy is still not full steam ahead, 9% growth doesn't seem too bad.

If I were considering Colgate-Palmolive, that ratio wouldn't scare me off if I liked the other attributes of the stock. Now, if next year the raise were only 2% and stayed low for another year, I might have to seriously consider whether this stock belongs in my portfolio.

If you prefer to calculate the dividend raises yourself, you can go to companies' websites—particularly those that have a long history of dividend increases. (They like to boast and give investors as much positive information as they can.) You will usually find a history of the company's dividends.

Simply calculate the rate that the company increased the dividend every year and average it out. You'll come up with the average growth rate. It might be helpful to see that dividend raise every year so that you can figure out what the numbers would have meant to you had you bought the stock X number of years ago.

For example, Table 7.3 is Brady Corp.'s (NYSE: BRC) dividend history (adjusted for a 2:1 stock split) over the last 10 years.

You can see that in 2005, the company raised its dividend from $0.425 to $0.46, or 8.2%. Then in 2006, the dividend was increased to $0.53, or 15.2%, and so on. Over the course of 10 years, the average raise was 6.6%.

You can also further see that the rate of the dividend increase slowed dramatically after 2009. From 2010 to 2013, the dividend

Table 7.3   Brady Corp.'s Dividend History

Year	Dividend	% Raise
2004	$0.425	4.9%
2005	$0.46	8.2%
2006	$0.53	15.2%
2007	$0.57	7.5%
2008	$0.62	8.8%
2009	$0.685	10.5%
2010	$0.705	2.9%
2011	$0.725	2.8%
2012	$0.745	2.8%
2013	$0.765	2.7%
Average		**6.6%**

Source: Brady Corp.

boost never went above 3%. If you'd owned the stock for a number of years, somewhere around 2012, you might've seriously taken a look at what was going on and why the annual dividend raise had slowed to a crawl.

Is it a new policy? Is the payout ratio too high? Has cash flow dried up? Once you understand the various pieces of information, you'll be better equipped to decide if you're going to keep the stock in your portfolio or punt it and move on to something else.

Companies don't always post their entire history of dividends; sometimes they choose to just show the past few years. But you can call the company's investor relations department to get the full data.

A free website, www.dividata.com, offers dividend history data as well. It has the dividend histories for most companies, although it doesn't go all the way back for every company.

For example, the site has data on Genuine Auto Parts (NYSE: GPC) going back to 1983, although the company has raised its dividend every year since 1956.

In Johnson & Johnson's (J&J) case, the data goes back to 1970, whereas J&J's own investor relations page on its corporate site goes back only to 1972.

If you want to see all of the dividends going back 30 or 40 years just for fun, knock yourself out. But it's not really relevant to whether the stock is an appropriate investment today. It doesn't matter that the company raised its dividend 11% in 1971. What we're most interested in is the past few years because that is likely the best indicator of what we can expect in the near future.

Of course, things can change. A company can find itself with a hot product and see a meaningful increase in cash flow, which might spur management to grow the dividend more than it has in the past. Or the opposite might occur. The company goes through a slump, and the previous 10% dividend hikes get cut to just 1% (to keep its streak alive).

But, generally speaking, if you want an idea of which direction dividend growth is moving and how much growth you can anticipate, take a look at the last 1-, 3-, 5-, and 10-year averages for a ballpark figure.

It's a good measuring stick for how the company is performing. If over the past 1, 3, 5, and 10 years, a company has averaged at least 10% dividend growth, and then this year it climbs only 2%, you may want to take a hard look at it to assess whether it is likely to provide you with the growth in income that you desire.

If the following year it also hikes the dividend only by 2%, it might be time to pull the plug and find an alternative that offers much higher growth.

Special Dividends

A special dividend is exactly what it sounds like. It's a dividend that's, well, special. Any questions?

A special dividend is usually a one-time payment, often much more than the regular dividend.

Look at the dividend chart (Figure 7.3) and data (Figure 7.4) on American Eagle Outfitters (NYSE: AEO). You can see that in 2009

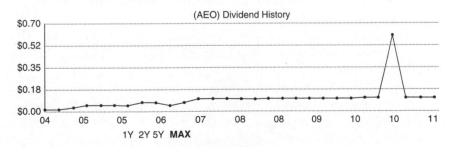

Figure 7.3 American Eagle Outfitters Dividend History

Source: Dividata.com

Ex-Dividend Date	Dividend Amount
Sep 22, 2011	$0.110000
Jul 6, 2011	$0.110000
Mar 24, 2011	$0.110000
Dec 9, 2010	$0.610000
Sep 23, 2010	$0.110000
Jun 24, 2010	$0.110000
Mar 25, 2010	$0.100000
Dec 23, 2009	$0.100000
Oct 7, 2009	$0.100000
Jul 1, 2009	$0.100000

Figure 7.4 Dividend Payment History for American Eagle Outfitters
Source: Dividata.com

through March 2010, American Eagle paid shareholders $0.10 per share quarterly. It raised the dividend to $0.11 in June 2010.

Then in December the dividend spiked to $0.61 but immediately went back down to $0.11.

On December 2, American Eagle declared a special $0.50 per share dividend on top of its regular $0.11 quarterly dividend. So shareholders received $0.61 per share that quarter.

A company may declare a special dividend for a number of reasons. One of the most common is because shareholders demand it. We saw that in 2004, when Microsoft, sitting on billions of dollars in cash, paid shareholders a special dividend of $3 per share. The payout barely put a dent in the company's cash stash but somewhat appeased investors, who were unhappy that the company was hoarding cash and not putting it to use acquiring other companies or for other growth initiatives.

Investors who demand special dividends do so because they feel that the company is holding *their* cash. If management isn't going to do something with it, the company might as well give it back.

As you can imagine, management rarely agrees with this opinion, but sometimes when the clamoring gets too loud, it throws investors a bone with a special dividend.

The reason I bring this up is because you don't want to include a special dividend in any annual dividend growth calculations. These are special one-time items. Unless the company specifies that it plans to give special dividends every year or so, you should not assume that you will receive another special dividend anytime soon.

Since distributing a special dividend is an abnormal event, including one in your dividend growth calculation would not give you an accurate picture of the company's dividend growth policy.

If you happen to own a stock that declares a special dividend, consider it gravy, a nice little extra bonus. But don't bank on one again. Instead, be sure you're invested in a company because it has an attractive yield and dividend growth rate based on its regular quarterly dividend.

Also, if you're calculating the payout ratio, be sure to remove the special dividend from your equation.

For example, if a company's regular annual dividend is $1 per share, it declared a special dividend of $0.50 per share during the year, and there are 100 million shares outstanding, the dividends paid should equal $150 million ($1.50 × 100 million).

When determining whether the payout ratio is sustainable, remove the $50 million, and base your calculation on the regular dividend, which totaled $100 million.

One last thing, though: Do look at the total dividends paid, *including* the special dividend, to make sure they don't exceed the company's cash flow.

If a company has 100 million shares, has a regular dividend of $1 per share, and declares a special dividend of $3, you should be concerned if the company's cash flow totals only $200 million.

The $100 million in regular dividends would have been fine from a payout ratio standpoint, as it equals only 50%. But with the special dividend of $300 million ($3 per share × 100 million shares), the total dividend paid is $400 million—$200 million more than the company's cash flow.

You want to make sure the company has a war chest of cash to pay that special dividend and that it's not borrowing money or selling shares to pay it.

Occasionally, a powerful hedge fund or investor will force a company to borrow money to pay a hefty dividend. If the dividend is not sustainable, the company is not one you want to be invested in for the long term.

Make sure you know where the cash is coming from to pay that special dividend.

Summary

- Diversify your holdings within a dividend portfolio.
- Don't invest for income according to how much money you need or when the dividend is paid; invest in quality companies with strong dividend performance.
- When looking at payout ratios, use cash flow.
- Know your stocks' dividend growth rates.
- I make a great baked ziti (I really do).

Note

1. "S&P 500 Dividend Year by Year," accessed November 17, 2014, http://www.multpl.com/s-p-500-dividend-yield/table.

The 10–11–12 System

Now it's time to put all of this knowledge to work and create a portfolio that is going to generate increasing amounts of annual income and create real wealth over the years.

The three important criteria in picking dividend stocks that, in 10 years, will generate 11% yields and 12% average annual total returns are:

- Yield
- Dividend growth
- Payout ratio

Yield

As we discussed, you don't want to chase yield. Never buy a stock simply because its yield is attractive. That being said, yield is a critical component of investing in dividend stocks. Starting out with a high enough yield will be vital to reaching your goals.

Just as, on one end of the spectrum, you wouldn't buy a stock with a 10% yield that was not growing or was unsustainable, you also wouldn't buy a low-yielding stock just because it was growing the dividend rapidly and the dividend appeared safe.

A low yielder might be attractive if it's a stock you're interested in for capital growth (you think the stock price is going significantly higher), but you wouldn't buy it for income.

Obviously, any stock you buy, even if it's for income purposes, you'll buy because you think that, over the long haul, its price will rise.

If you think a company is a dog in an obsolete industry, you probably don't want to own it regardless of its historical dividend increases. If you believe the company is in trouble, you won't be able to sleep at night. And letting you sleep at night is exactly what the kind of stocks I'm talking about in this book are designed to do.

A company with a 1.4% dividend yield that has a low payout ratio and is raising its dividend by 10% per year is not going to get you where you want to be.

Even with a 10% dividend boost every year, your yield will only be 3.3% in 10 years.

That's not a terrible yield to start out with today, but we want much more than that 10 years from now.

Dividend Growth

The stock market is all about growth. Investors buy stocks whose earnings and cash flow are growing. Income investors want rising dividends. CEOs try to grow their sales and margins. Investors pay higher prices for companies that are growing. If a company stops growing, its stock price usually gets hammered.

A key component in the formula is dividend growth. Without it, the dividend will lose its buying power because of inflation. Even with low inflation, over the years, the money won't buy as much as it used to.

A company that raises its dividend by a meaningful amount every year typically has rising earnings and cash flow. It's a sign of a healthy business and, just as important, shows that management understands its fiduciary duty to shareholders.

The historical average dividend growth of the S&P 500 is 5.5% per year. That's not bad, considering the average inflation rate of 3.4%. Using historical averages, that means investors are getting 2.1% more buying power each year. So investing in the S&P 500 has kept investors ahead of inflation and preserves their buying power.

But we want to be way ahead of inflation. Inflation isn't always going to stay low. In some areas of the economy, it's already pretty darn high. Gas, food, and college tuition are just a few segments where prices seem to rise significantly every year, no matter what government statistics say.

Therefore, we want strong (but sustainable) growth in our dividend every year.

Payout Ratio

It's all about safety. Before you dive in and pick great stocks that will generate huge amounts of money, you want to ensure that the stocks will stay great and help you meet your financial goals. If the company's finances are not in good shape, it's likely to disappoint you sometime down the road. So be sure the company can continue with its dividend policy.

Warren Buffett's first rule of investing is "Don't lose money." His second rule is "Don't forget rule number 1."

Dividend investors should heed Buffett's words. For the compounding machine to gain momentum every year, the dividend needs to grow. If the company can't maintain dividend growth and has to slash the dividend, that derails the train (and likely the stock price). You'll most likely have to sell your stock at a lower price and start over with a new one.

By looking at a company's payout ratio, you can usually avoid most of the problem stocks that could lead a portfolio off the rails.

Remember, generally speaking I want to see payout ratios (based on cash flow) of 75% or less, unless the stock is a BDC, REIT, or MLP. In those cases they can be as high as 100% of cash flow since many of them have policies to pay out all or nearly all of their cash flow, although in those cases the margin of safety is much lower. It might only take a difficult year or two to disrupt an annual dividend growth streak.

Formula

To achieve 11% yields and 12% average annual returns in 10 years, we'll need to make some assumptions. We'll also change those assumptions so that you can see what you'll need to alter to obtain the 10–11–12 results you're looking for.

As I stated earlier in the book, I don't believe in dogma. Anyone who tells you that you should never, or always, buy a stock above or below a certain valuation, yield, payout ratio, technical indicator, et cetera, is lying either to you or to themself.

That's a pretty strong statement, considering how many people out there profess to have all of the answers to the investment world. But the markets just don't work that way.

Stocks have a tendency to stay overbought or oversold, to move farther in a direction than most investors are prepared for. The market is a living, breathing animal that has a mind of its own and doesn't concern itself with gurus' hard-and-fast rules.

That said, we can still use guidelines to shape our strategy and use historical figures and averages as points of reference. Very often stocks do revert to the mean, so if you buy stocks trading below their historical average price–earnings (P/E) ratios, chances are, somewhere down the road, the stocks will trade at that historical average once again.

Keep all of this in mind as I give you guidelines for the stocks that will create a great portfolio of income-producing assets designed to provide you with a yield of 11% and generate an average annual total return of 12% within 10 years.

If you discover a stock that you like but it is two-tenths of a percentage point below my suggested minimum yield, remember, the rules are not set in stone. If the payout ratio is 3% too high but you have good reason to believe earnings and cash flow growth will be strong over the next few years, go for it. These numbers are meant to be a guide. They're good ones, but they're only a guide.

Before I give you those guidelines, here are those assumptions.

Assumption 1. Unless otherwise stated, over the next 10 years, the stock will appreciate 7.84% per year, equal to the historical average of the stock market since 1961.

That 7.84% return includes the Great Recession, various market crashes, and run-of-the-mill bear markets. It also includes good times, like the bull market of the 1990s and the 2010s.

I know there are lots of bears out there who believe this time it's different. That our country and the world has dug itself a hole so deep, it will never be able to get out of it.

In the first edition of this book, which was written in late 2011, the previous paragraph concluded this way: "Maniacal world leaders now have nuclear weapons, housing isn't likely to bounce back soon, we're running out of oil, and every other scary thing out there is going to cause the stock market to fall."

Interesting that only three years later two of those problems are gone. Unfortunately, there are still maniacs with terrible weapons. But housing has bounced back and the United States is now flush with oil and other cheap energy.

Of course, there are other problems we can still point to: terrorists running rampant in the Middle East, crushing debt, economies around the world still limping along, global warming and the rising oceans. ...

There are still lots of scary things out there that could cause the market to go down, including the fact that as I write this we're more than five and a half years into a bull market.

So maybe the market will fall. I don't forecast the market. What I do know is that we've had some pretty bad times before. While Hitler's army caused unspeakable carnage in Europe and 60 million people—2.5% of the world's population—died during World War II, the stock market performed extremely well.

As I mentioned earlier, in 76 rolling 10-year periods, the market has been negative only 7 times. There has been a lot of calamity in those 86 years. Wars, assassinations, civil unrest, scandals, shortages, and horrible political leadership—and through it all the market was positive 91% of the time after 10 years, and significantly positive, at that. On average, investors more than doubled their money every 10 years in the market.

Yes, the world has some problems right now. Some are extremely serious. But I'm going to side with history and assume that the next 10, 20, and 30 years are going to be similar to the last 50—and that stocks will rise in line with their average of 7.84%.

And keep in mind that dividend stocks, particularly those with solid yields that are growing their dividends, historically have outperformed the market. So our 7.84% assumption may be conservative. I don't think it's unreasonable to expect a 9% or 10% average annual price increase from these types of stocks if the general market is hitting its average of 7.84%.

I'll run some scenarios where the market underperforms the average and even some where the market stays flat or loses money to show you how the formula performs in all types of markets.

Assumption 2. The averages are consistent. In the financial model that we've built to analyze these prospective portfolios, we have to assume that the average stock performance and dividend growth is consistent. That will certainly not be the case in real life.

Even if stocks go up an average of 7.84% per year over the next 10 years, your stock is obviously not going to do that every single year. It might rise 10% this year, rise 5% the next, fall 4% the following, be flat, climb 20%, and so on. Those price moves will have an impact on your total returns.

If you're reinvesting your dividends for the long haul, the best-case scenario is actually a weak stock market where your company is still growing earnings and dividends. That way you get to reinvest the dividends at lower prices. The only time you should care about the stock price climbing is if you want to sell. If not, let your stock stay in the dumps and be undervalued—as long as the dividend is growing and sustainable.

It feels very contrary to every emotion we've ever had about the market, but I actually get annoyed when one of my dividend stocks goes higher.

If one of my stocks popped over 10% after strong earnings and a dividend hike announcement, now instead of reinvesting my dividends at around $29 per share, I have to reinvest at $33. It's nice to have a $4 gain in the stock, but it doesn't really matter to me now since I'm not planning on selling it for 20 years. I'd rather have it be at $29 (or $25) so that I can buy more shares every time a dividend is issued.

We have to model the averages as a consistent number because we have no idea how the market will play out, even if it does perform according to averages.

You can play with the dividend calculator, which is available for free on the Get Rich with Dividends website at www .getrichwithdividends.com, and change the variables to see how the investment will perform when the inputs change. You can also access a dividend calculator at www.wealthyretirement, which is the site for my free e-letter, *Wealthy Retirement,* and is available at www.wealthyretirement.com.

If you're especially bearish or bullish, try to resist tinkering with the average return of the stock. Even the professionals—or, I should say, *especially* the professionals—get it wrong. How many times have you seen a previously bullish analyst downgrade a stock after the company missed earnings and the stock cratered? How many times have you seen a prominent Wall Street money manager be completely wrong on the direction he predicted stocks were going to move?

It happens all the time, so do yourself a favor and stick with the averages. If you want to change the average to see what happens in bullish or bearish scenarios, that's fine (and I'll do that for you in the pages that follow), but resist the urge to change the stock's price each year based on what you think is going to happen.

Ditto for the dividend growth figures.

So, here's the moment you've been waiting for: instructions on how to set up your own 10–11–12 portfolio.

As they say, "Safety first." The first item we're going to look at is designed to keep your portfolio safe and to ensure that the stocks you buy will continue to be able to pay and grow their dividend.

Payout Ratio: 75% or Lower

Not including REITs, BDCs, and MLPs, I look for companies whose payout ratios are 75% or lower, with growing sales, earnings, and cash flow. Of any of the guidelines, this is probably the one you want to stick to the closest, because we're talking about the stability of the dividend. If you go outside the boundaries on yield or dividend growth and things don't work out right, you may make a little less money than you thought.

But if the dividend is cut, chances are your stock is going to fall, maybe significantly. And you probably won't want to be invested in it anymore and may sell for a loss.

In this entire strategy, the reliability of the dividend is the most important factor. If you're relying on dividends for income, you may not be able to afford a cut.

A reduction in dividends may set a wealth-building program back a bit, which wouldn't be as devastating as it may be to the investor who needs the dividends to meet living expenses, but it still would be a hindrance to achieving your goals.

Of course, if you find a stock with a payout ratio of 50%, you have plenty of margin for error. Even if business stinks and earnings fall, there should be plenty of cash to continue to pay the dividend.

Should that happen, keep a close eye on the payout ratio. Management may be reluctant to cut the dividend, especially if the company has a long track record of raises. But if earnings are on a downtrend and the payout ratio is increasing, management may be forced to lower the dividend paid to shareholders. If the payout ratio starts moving higher, it may be a hint that a cut or a halt to the raises is coming.

Ultimately, you'd like to be invested in a company with sales, earnings, and especially cash flow that are on the rise. With a reasonable payout ratio, that gives management plenty of room to continue to increase the dividend.

Don't get bent out of shape if the company has a bad year or two, particularly if the payout ratio is low enough that the dividend isn't threatened. But if a company has year after year of negative sales, earnings, or cash flow growth, you might want to start looking elsewhere. It's not going to be the healthiest company, even if the payout ratio is low and the dividend continues to grow.

In a perfect world, I'd like to see 10% or more growth in sales, earnings, and cash flow, but that is not always easy to find, particularly in mature, stable companies that have a long history of dividend growth. So be sure to keep an eye on the company and look for at least some growth in those areas.

By following the payout ratio and noticing that it's redlining (75%+), particularly if it has risen in a hurry, you should be able to bail out before things hit the fan.

Let's look at an example of a company that cut its dividend and see whether we could see any warning signs.

Table 8.1 and Figure 8.1 show the dividends paid out by Vulcan Materials Company (NYSE: VMC), which cut its quarterly dividend in half in the third quarter of 2009 to $0.25 from $0.49 per share. I've included the payout ratios based on net income, cash flow from operations, and free cash flow.

Free cash flow: Cash flow from operations minus capital expenditures. Including capital expenditures as a cost of doing business on the cash flow statement makes sense because it is cash that is being spent to run or grow the business.

Could we have foreseen a cut coming?

Table 8.1　Vulcan Materials Company's Payout Ratios (Dollar Amounts in Millions)

	2004	2005	2006	2007	2008	2009	2010
Dividends	$106	$118	$144	$181	$215	$171	$128
Net income	287	389	468	451	(4)	30	96
Payout ratio	37%	30%	31%	40%	NM	570%	133%
Cash flow/operations	$581	$473	$579	$708	$435	$453	$203
Payout ratio	18%	25%	25%	26%	50%	38%	63%
Free cash flow	$377	$258	$144	$225	$82	$343	$116
Payout ratio	28%	46%	100%	80%	262%	50%	110%

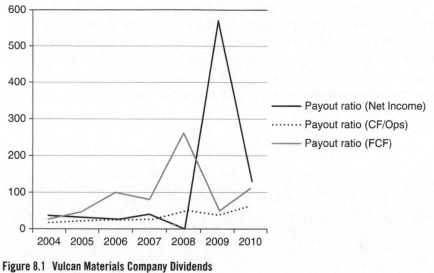

Figure 8.1 Vulcan Materials Company Dividends

Source: Chart: Marc Lichtenfeld; Data: Morningstar

You can see that the payout ratios, according to net income and cash flow from operations, were all in a very safe area until 2008, when, because of a net loss, the payout ratio based on earnings is not meaningful (and falls to zero on the chart). Based on cash flow from operations, it was still 50%, which is normally fairly stable. However, this sudden doubling of the payout ratio rather than a nice steady trend upward should have set off some alarm bells.

Free cash flow gave us a warning even earlier, when the payout ratio hit 100% of free cash flow in 2006. That should have put investors on alert. Dropping down to 80% in 2007 may have changed it to a code yellow from code red, but shareholders still ought to have been watching it carefully. Then in 2008, dividends exceeded free cash flow. At that point, investors should've thought very carefully about whether Vulcan was a stock that still belonged in their portfolios.

Of course, 2008 was when the financial crisis hit, and it was a bad year for everyone. But the sudden pops in the payout ratio served as a warning that the dividend was in jeopardy.

Notice that the dividend wasn't cut until the second half of 2009. When things get bad, management typically is reactive instead of proactive. It will try hard not to cut the dividend even if bad earnings numbers are expected. Companies often wait until the last possible minute to avoid further angering shareholders, who might already be steamed by the weak profits and performance of the stock.

Very often, the warning signs are there a few quarters before the cut occurs, giving vigilant investors time to make changes to their portfolios.

Vulcan's fourth-quarter 2011 dividend was cut to $0.01 from $0.25. That's no surprise, considering:

Payout ratio on net income: not meaningful—the company has been profitable in only one of the last eight quarters.

Payout ratio on cash flow from operations: 65%, up slightly from 2010s spike.

Payout ratio on free cash flow: 135%, up 25 percentage points from 2010s already-high level.

Analysis on the payout ratio should have kept any dividend investor out of the stock regardless of its yield, which was 3.2% before the cut.

Occasionally, a company will state a payout ratio policy in a quarterly report, annual report, or earnings conference call. The payout ratio goal is usually based on earnings of free cash flow.

That's worth paying close attention to. If the company does not grow its earnings or free cash flow, dividend growth could be in trouble, or the payout ratio is climbing higher than management originally intended. Listen to or read the transcripts from the company's earnings conference calls to see if the CEO or CFO mentions the change in the payout ratio policy. That way you can assess whether management is doing the right thing for the business or whether you need to get out while the gettin's still good.

On the other hand, if earnings and free cash flow are growing and the company has a stated payout ratio policy, the dividend should grow along with it. If it doesn't, again, listen for any changes in the policy.

In its third quarter 2014 earnings call, the CEO of Covanta Holding Corporation (NYSE: CVA) said his company was targeting a 50% payout ratio based on free cash flow. He added that the goal is to grow free cash flow so that it can be reinvested into the business to grow it even more and maintain that 50% payout ratio, lifting the dividend along with it.

As a shareholder, that free cash flow figure would be something I'd keep an eye on—not too closely, however. Remember, we don't want to overtrade and react to every variation in every quarter. We're long-term investors so we're going to let some things work themselves out and smooth out over time. But if you see after a year that the payout ratio is too high, and after another year or two it hasn't dipped back to that 50% mark, then it might be time to look for another investment.

On the other hand, if free cash flow is growing strong and the payout ratio is below 50%, you might expect that a big dividend increase is coming.

If management mentions a payout ratio goal, pay attention to it and follow it over time.

Yield: 4.7% or Higher

You might be reading this book in 2030 after your parents or grandparents insisted on it because it made a huge difference in their financial well-being.

It's the reason your parents are able to send you to that fancy school of yours, why you live in the nice house with the two jetpacks in the garage, or why Mom goes on cruises every year in retirement.

I can see into the future and believe those things really can come true by following the ideas in this book.

What I can't see is where interest rates will be in the future. In 2030, you might be getting 17% in your savings account. A mortgage might be 22%. I have no idea.

In the current low-interest-rate environment, a 4.7% yield on a stable company is pretty solid. You can go down to 4% if you need to, especially because as investors have started searching in earnest for yield, they have been buying up the dividend-paying stocks, sending the yields lower.

But even that 0.7% difference, which seems pretty small, can make a significant impact on your portfolio.

For example, if you own a stock with a 4.7% yield that increases the dividend by 10% every year, after 10 years, your yield will be 11.1%. Using the same growth scenario but starting with a 4% yield, your yield a decade later will be 9.4%. On a $10,000 initial investment, you'll collect $1,100 more in dividends over the 10 years with the 4.7% yielder than you will with the 4% stock.

If you reinvest the dividends, after 10 years, the stock with the 4.7% yield will be worth $20,993 (assuming no price movement of the stock) versus $18,815 when you start at 4%.

So you can see, even with a stock yielding 4%, the results aren't bad over the long haul. You still end up with a 9.4% yield on your original investment, and, if you reinvest the dividends, your investment grows by 88% (again, assuming no stock price movement). But that 0.7% does add up over time.

Remember, 4.7% is not a hard-and-fast rule, but it's above the historical average annual U.S. inflation rate of 3.4% since 1914.

So, in today's current low-interest-rate environment, a 4.7% starting yield should be enough of a buffer above inflation to ensure you're not losing purchasing power. And then by starting above the inflation rate, as long as the dividend grows, you should be able to stay ahead of inflation over the years.

Of course, there could be a few outlier years, as we experienced in the late 1970s when inflation soared into the double digits. If you own dividend stocks with decent starting yields and strong annual dividend growth, it's quite possible you'll stay ahead of even abnormal inflation rates.

A stock with a 4% yield that grows by 10% per year will yield double digits by year 11 and will yield 20% by year 18. And if the stock, on average, climbs higher, just a little, your average annual returns will be in the low to mid-teens after 10 years and significantly higher after 15 and 20. So, if your time horizon is long enough, chances are you'll have nothing to worry about even in a high-inflation environment. In 10 years if you're earning 11% yields, which are growing by double digits, even if inflation were at a historically high 8% or 9%, you'd have nothing to worry about. I'm not saying it would be pleasant, but your purchasing power would not erode.

And if inflation stays anywhere near historical norms, imagine how happy you'll be with an 11% to 20% yield down the road.

As a rule of thumb, try to find stocks yielding at least 4%, although 4.7% is the goal. If you can't find one or you discover a stock you like but the yield is too low, you can wait for it to come down while you search for others. Or, if you're comfortable with put selling, sell puts on it and collect income while you wait for the stock to reach the price you'd like to buy it at. We talk about options in Chapter 10.

Dividend Growth: 10% or Higher

There aren't that many companies out there with dividend growth of 10% or more. In fact, out of the 346 companies that have raised their dividends every year for the past 10 years, only 162 have boosted the dividend by an average of 10% per year for that 10-year period.

Obviously, you'd like as much growth as you can possibly get. But it's okay to sacrifice a little bit of growth for a higher starting yield—providing that the dividend is safe. It is *not* okay to buy a stock with a 13% yield that is unsustainable.

But if you start out with a higher yield, you can give up a few percentage points of annual growth. Of course, there's no guarantee of what future growth will be; we can only go off what the company has done in the past and any statements it has made regarding dividend policy.

For example, in an earnings or dividend announcement, the company might state that it remains committed to 9% to 10% dividend growth for the foreseeable future.

Again, no guarantees, but that should give you a good frame of reference on which to base your forecast.

If you can't find any stated dividend policy in a company's press releases or corporate presentations on its website, call investor relations and ask whether it has one.

Take a look at what happens if we increase the starting yield but lower the growth forecast. We'll assume we invested $10,000 and the stock price never moves. (See Table 8.2.)

As you go farther out to 15 and 20 years, the stocks with the higher growth rate surpass those with the higher starting yield and lower growth rate. See Table 8.3.

Table 8.2   Growth Is Important, but a Decent Starting Yield Is, Too

Yield	Dividend Growth Rate	Yield Year 5	Yield Year 10	Value with Reinvested Dividends Year 5	Value with Reinvested Dividends Year 10
4%	10%	5.9%	9.4%	$12,746	$18,815
4.5%	9%	6.4%	9.8%	$13,066	$19,690
5%	8%	6.8%	10%	$13,379	$20,493

Table 8.3   In Later Years, Dividend Growth Is More Important Than Starting Yield

Yield	Dividend Growth Rate	Yield Year 15	Yield Year 20	Value with Reinvested Dividends Year 15	Value with Reinvested Dividends Year 20
4%	10%	15.2%	24.5%	$35,096	$94,880
4.5%	9%	15.0%	23.1%	$36,878	$96,058
5%	8%	14.7%	21.8%	$38,224	$94,891

Also, it's interesting to note that reinvesting dividends for 20 years achieves the same results with a 4% starting yield and 10% dividend growth as you get with a 5% starting yield with only 8% growth.

So in this case, higher dividend growth made up for the lower starting yield. And it certainly did when you don't reinvest dividends and simply look at what the yields turn into by compounding the growth rate.

Of course, no stock is static, so the fluctuations in the stock price will influence the value after reinvesting dividends.

But these tables are here to show you that while dividend growth is very important to keep up with inflation and serve as the fuel for the compounding machine, you also need a decent starting yield to get the process moving.

Certainly look for a 10% growth rate, but don't sweat it if you can't find exactly what you're searching for. Since the growth rate will fluctuate depending on management's decisions, what it will be is really not completely knowable. The starting yield is certain, however, and the past payout ratio that signals whether the dividend is safe is also known.

You need the growth to make this process work, but put a bit more weight on the yield and payout ratio.

It also helps to have a company that is growing earnings and cash flow. As you saw from the section on payout ratio, to continue to increase the dividend without getting into dangerous territory, the company needs to increase the pool of money from which it is paying dividends.

Even with a low payout ratio, a company whose earnings and cash flow have stalled will have a difficult time justifying a dividend raise year after year. You don't need superhot growth. Even single-digit growth often will suffice to ensure there is enough cash to grow the dividend by a meaningful amount every year.

Numbers

In the next tables, I'll lay out for you what starting yield you need to reach the 10–11–12 goals based on various dividend growth and price appreciation assumptions.

Table 8.4 and the tables to follow show the yield and the amount of dividend income if dividends are not reinvested. The next two rows are the yield on original cost and yearly dividends if dividends are reinvested. The last two rows are the compound annual growth rate and total value, so you can see that we're hitting our goal of 12%.

Below Table 8.4 and the rest of the tables is a list of the assumptions we're making. So in this one we have average market performance of 7.84%, 10% annual dividend growth, a $10,000 starting investment, and a 4.7% starting yield.

The assumptions are the basic formula. Assume that over the next 10 years, the market is going to appreciate the same amount as its historical average. Next, find a stock with a dividend growth rate of 10% (that is likely to continue at that rate) and a starting yield of 4.7%.

You can see that in 10 years, we've achieved the 11% yield when dividends are not reinvested and a 13% average annual return when dividends are reinvested. Also notice that when dividends are

Table 8.4   Average Market with 10% Dividend Growth

	5 Years	10 Years	15 Years	20 Years
Yield (dividends not reinvested)	6.9%	11.1%	17.8%	28.7%
Annual income	$688	$1,108	$1,784	$2,874
Yield on original investment (dividends reinvested)	8.64%	18.08%	38.88%	86.17%
Annual income (dividends reinvested)	$864	$1,808	$3,888	$8,617
Compound annual growth rate (CAGR)	13.11%	13.39%	13.69%	14.02%
Total value	$18,517	$35,147	$68,555	$137,800

Assumptions:
Average market with 10% dividend growth.
$10,000 investment.
Annual stock price appreciation: 7.84% (historical average).
Annual dividend growth rate: 10%.
Necessary starting yield: 4.7%.

Table 8.5   Weak Market with 10% Dividend Growth

	5 Years	10 Years	15 Years	20 Years
Yield (dividends not reinvested)	7.8%	12.5%	20.1%	32.4%
Annual income	$776	$1,249	$2,012	$3,241
Yield on original investment (dividends reinvested)	9.9%	22.7%	56.8%	159.4%
Annual income	$993	$2,271	$5,684	$15,944
CAGR	11.18%	12.01%	12.99%	14.14%
Total value	$16,987	$31,079	$62,421	$140,933

Assumptions:
Weak market with 10% dividend growth.
$10,000 investment.
Annual stock price appreciation: 5% (below historical average).
Annual dividend growth rate: 10%.
Necessary starting yield: 5.3%.

reinvested, the yield on your original investment is now nearly 18% rather than 11%.

In Table 8.5, we're modeling a slower market than usual. Even if you're somewhat bearish, this is a safe assumption as the market has been up 67 out of 74 times over the past three-quarters of a century. If we hit a bear market during some part of the next decade, chances are we'll still finish the 10-year period up. A 5% annual stock market return would be a pretty big disappointment for most investors.

Notice in this scenario that you need a higher starting yield to make up for the weak market. To reach our goals, you'll have to start out with a 5.3% yield and hit the 10% dividend growth numbers.

If you do, you'll have a 12.5% yield in 10 years, or 22% if the dividends are reinvested. That's because you're reinvesting the dividends at lower stock prices than in the first scenario, buying more shares with a higher dividend per share. As compounding works its magic, it will result in a greater return as the years go by.

After 10 years, your return in percentage and total dollars is a bit lower than in the first scenario, but after 20, all those cheap shares you bought add up and generate a 14% return.

In Table 8.6, we're planning for another decade like the one we had recently, the 10-year period known as the lost decade. From 2002 to 2011, the return of the S&P 500 was, to use a technical term, bubkes. It averaged less than 1% per year.

Table 8.6   Nowhere Market with 10% Dividend Growth

	5 Years	10 Years	15 Years	20 Years
Yield (dividends not reinvested)	10.5%	17%	27.3%	44%
Annual income	$1,054	$1,697	$2,734	$4,403
Yield on cost (dividends reinvested)	15.3%	47.4%	217.7%	1,853%
Annual income	$1,526	$4,742	$21,796	$185,309
CAGR	9.08%	11.97%	16.09%	22.1%
Total value	$15,445	$30,962	$93,791	$542,675

Assumptions:
Nowhere market, 10% dividend growth.
$10,000 investment.
Annual stock price appreciation: 0%.
Annual dividend growth rate: 10%.
Necessary starting yield: 7.2%.

If you invested your money on December 31, 2001, and didn't look at it again until 10 years later, you had no idea what a wild ride it was. All you'd see is that your portfolio barely budged.

In the next 10 years, we're going to assume the market is slightly worse and doesn't return a penny. That $10,000 invested in the S&P 500 is worth $10,000 a decade later.

But look, even with a flat market, strong returns are possible. You'll have to find a stock yielding 7.2% to hit our numbers, but it can be done.

For what it's worth, if you invested in an easier-to-find stock yielding 4.7% that grew its dividend 10% per year in a flat market, you'll still get that 11% yield after 10 years, or nearly 22% if you reinvested the dividends. And your average annual return would be 7.7%, which would more than double your money.

I don't think anyone would complain about that. Would you have complained about a 7.7% annual return on your portfolio between 2002 and 2011? Probably not. If the market returned zero but you got 7.7%, you'd probably be thrilled at your good fortune.

In Table 8.7, I chose an average annual return of −1.2% because that was the average for the 10-year periods that were negative. It's certainly possible that we could experience an even worse decline, but considering how few times negative returns occurred, I believe the average is a safe assumption.

Look how high the numbers get, particularly beyond 10 years, when you reinvest the dividend. That's when the compounding machine really begins to gather momentum.

Table 8.7   Bear Market with 10% Dividend Growth

	5 Years	10 Years	15 Years	20 Years
Yield (dividends not reinvested)	11.0%	17.7%	28.5%	45.9%
Annual income	$1,098	$1,768	$2,848	$4,586
Yield on original investment (dividends reinvested)	16.3%	55.1%	311.2%	4,099.7%
Annual income	$1,630	$5,514	$31,122	$409,969
CAGR	8.45%	12.03%	17.42%	25.72%
Total value	$15,003	$31,142	$111,273	$973,662

Assumptions:
Bear market, 10% dividend growth.
$10,000 investment.
Annual stock price appreciation: −1.2% (historical average of 10-year negative rolling returns).
Annual dividend growth rate: 10%.
Necessary starting yield: 7.5%.

The fact that the stock price is declining allows the investor to buy more shares at a lower price. Those lower-priced shares still generate significant income, which is being put right back to work in more lower-priced shares. As a result, the investor accumulates a ton of shares, which, even with the lower stock price, becomes worth a significant amount of money.

Imagine if we hit a bear market so rough that, for 20 years, the average return of the market was negative (that has never happened, by the way), and you turned your $10,000 original investment into nearly $1 million. To say you'd be ecstatic would be an understatement.

Reality check: If we hit a sustained bear market that delivered annual negative returns over the course of 20 years, it might be difficult, even for the best Perpetual Dividend Raisers, to continue raising their dividends at 10% per year. But keep in mind that during the Great Recession years of 2008 and 2009, plenty of companies continued to raise their dividends at double-digit paces.

I have no doubt that during the next long and significant decline in the market, many companies will find a way to raise the dividend, even if it's just a few percentage points as a token amount to keep their records intact. In January 2012, Kimberly-Clark (NYSE: KMB) raised its dividend for the 40th consecutive year, which includes the Great Recession of 2008 and 2009.

Kimberly-Clark had been raising the dividend around 9% to 10% per year, including 9.4% in 2008. However, in 2009, it tapped on the

Table 8.8   1,000 Shares Reinvested Grow to . . .

Stock Performance	10 Years	20 Years
10%	1,578	2,492
7.84%	1,652	3,045
5%	1,774	4,404
0%	2,099	13,922
−1.2%	2,209	21,443

brakes and raised the dividend by only 3.4%. In 2010, however, it was right back to a 10% raise.

As long as the dividend is growing, you'll still acquire lots more shares, which will increase the value of your holdings significantly, not to mention the income should you decide to stop reinvesting.

To illustrate the power of compounding, even in a bear market, look at how many shares you'd have at the end of 10 and 20 years based on the first example, where the starting yield is 4.7% and the dividend grows 10% per year. (See Table 8.8.)

I'm sure it jumps out at you how many more shares you have the worse the stock performs. It's astonishing to think that a sustained bear market would make you richer than a bull market.

In the first 5 to 10 years, that's not so. The bull market wins. But as the compounding magnifies, you're buying hundreds or even thousands of shares per quarter. And even at lower stock prices, all those shares add up to make you wealthy.

Another thing to consider: If we are unfortunate enough to experience a 20-year bear market or at least a market where the average annual return is negative over 20 years, chances are that inflation will be very low.

That would make your returns even more valuable. If you turned $10,000 into even a few hundred thousand dollars during that kind of economy, you probably would not lose much if anything to inflation. And I guarantee that if you turn $10,000 into several hundred thousand dollars during a 20-year bear market, you'd do better than 99% of the people out there.

From 1929 to 1941, prices declined by an average of 1% per year. And that includes the 5% inflation rate of 1941, when the war effort was kicking into gear.

Table 8.9   Bull Market with 10% Dividend Growth

	5 Years	10 Years	15 Years	20 Years
Yield (dividends not reinvested)	6.9%	11%	17.8%	28.7%
Annual income	$688	$1,108	$1,784	$2,874
Yield on cost (dividends reinvested)	$840	$1,701	$3,442	$6,967
Annual income	8.4%	17%	34.4%	69.7%
Average annual return	15.14%	15.14%	15.14%	15.14%
Total value	$20,236	$40,951	$82,870	$167,700

Assumptions:
Bull market, 10% dividend growth.
$10,000 investment.
Stock price appreciation: 10% (above historical average).
Dividend growth rate: 10%.
Necessary starting yield: 4.7%.

So, if we experienced deflation, where prices are falling, your dividend windfall would actually be worth even more in real purchasing power.

Next, we look at a strong market. Interestingly, in Table 8.9 you'll notice the average annual return when you reinvest the dividends stays constant. That's because the growth rates of both variables are the same.

You also see that your $10,000 quadruples to $40,000 in this bull market when you reinvest the dividends. And after 20 years, your yearly dividends are equal to 70% of your original investment.

A 10% dividend growth rate is the goal, but we might not always be able to achieve it. Let's look at some of the similar scenarios with 5% dividend growth instead, so you have an idea as to what kind of returns you can expect at the lower growth rate.

The first thing that jumps out about the calculations in Table 8.10 is that the average annual return is actually declining—not the value of the investment. Your money is still growing. But the annual return is slowing. That's because the dividend growth rate is lower than the stock price appreciation. The increasing dividends that you're receiving are not keeping pace with the rising cost of the stock.

For example, in the fourth quarter of year 5, your reinvested dividend buys 12.1 shares at $14.58 (initial purchase price is $10). Five years later, in the last quarter of year 10, you'll buy 12.8 shares for $21.27. You're buying 6% more shares in year 10 but paying 46% more.

Table 8.10   Average Market with 5% Dividend Growth

	5 Years	10 Years	15 Years	20 Years
Yield (dividends not reinvested)	5.7%	7.3%	9.3%	11.9%
Annual income	$571	$729	$930	$1,187
Yield on original investment (dividends reinvested)	7.03%	10.88%	16.42%	24.27%
Annual income (dividends reinvested)	$703	$1,088	$1,642	$2,427
Average annual return	12.64%	12.33%	12.06%	11.80%
Total value	$18,131	$31,998	$55,147	$93,088

Assumptions:
Average market with 5% dividend growth.
$10,000 investment.
Annual stock price appreciation: 7.84% (historical average).
Annual dividend growth rate: 5%.
Necessary starting yield: 4.7%.

Think of it another way. The dividend growth rate is your increase in income, and the stock appreciation is the rate of inflation. You're getting a raise of 5% every year, but the cost of living (buying more shares) is increasing 7.84%, so your income, although it's going higher, is not keeping pace with the thing you want to buy (the stock). This isn't a bad thing as you're still compounding the dividends and increasing your wealth. There's nothing wrong with an 11.8% total return over 20 years, turning $10,000 into more than $93,000.

By comparing Tables 8.11, 8.12, 8.13, and 8.14 with the 5% dividend growth with those with the 10% growth, you can see that the difference in dividend growth rate certainly makes a difference, but not a huge one.

Again, even with slower dividend growth, $10,000 still grows by more than 11 times over 20 years when the market is negative.

For example, in the average market scenario with the 4.7% yield and 7.84% stock appreciation, after 10 years of reinvesting the dividend, the $10,000 original investment is worth $35,147 with 10% dividend growth and $31,998 with 5% dividend growth. The total returns were 13.39% and 12.33%, respectively.

As the years go by, the difference becomes more significant because of the effect of compounding. In a perfect world, you want a high starting yield and high dividend growth. Since that's not always achievable, try to come up with a combination of both, but be sure your original yield is high enough so that when compounding's

Table 8.11   Weak Market with 5% Dividend Growth

	5 Years	10 Years	15 Years	20 Years
Yield (dividends not reinvested)	6.4%	8.2%	10.5%	13.4%
Annual income	$644	$822	$1,049	$1,339
Yield on original investment (dividends reinvested)	8.1%	13.4%	22.2%	36.7%
Annual income	$809	$1,339	$2,218	$3,671
Average annual return	10.61%	10.61%	10.61%	10.61%
Total value	$16,554	$27,406	$45,371	$75,111

Assumptions:
Weak market with 5% dividend growth.
$10,000 investment.
Annual stock price appreciation: 5% (below historical average).
Annual dividend growth rate: 5%.
Necessary starting yield: 5.3%.

magic does kick in, there's a meaningful base that's high enough to help you achieve your goals.

One other note on the 5% dividend growth scenario: You need a 7.1% starting yield to achieve an 11% yield in 10 years. To get a 12% total return in 10 years with dividends reinvested, you'll need to see the stock appreciate an average of 5% per year.

When to Sell

I'd love to give you a definite rule for when to sell your positions when the stock doesn't cooperate, but as I said earlier, I don't believe that

Table 8.12   Nowhere Market with 5% Dividend Growth

	5 Years	10 Years	15 Years	20 Years
Yield (dividends not reinvested)	8.8%	11.1%	14.3%	18.2%
Annual income	$875	$1,116	$1,425	$1,819
Yield on cost (dividends reinvested)	12.3%	25.5%	60.6%	169.8%
Annual income	$1,229	$2,553	$6,054	$16,978
Average annual return	8.2%	9.37%	10.76%	12.43%
Total value	$14,827	$24,481	$46,322	$104,167

Assumptions:
Nowhere market, 5% dividend growth.
$10,000 investment.
Annual stock price appreciation: 0%.
Annual dividend growth rate: 5%.
Necessary starting yield: 7.2%.

Table 8.13   Bear Market with 5% Dividend Growth

	5 Years	10 Years	15 Years	20 Years
Yield (dividends not reinvested)	9.1%	11.6%	14.8%	19%
Annual income	$911	$1,163	$1,484	$1,895
Yield on original investment (dividends reinvested)	13.1%	28.97%	77.59%	268.79%
Annual income	$1,310	$2,896	$7,758	$26,878
Average annual return	7.5%	9.1%	11.1%	13.6%
Total value	$14,355	$23,892	$48,512	$128,567

Assumptions:
Bear market, 5% dividend growth.
$10,000 investment.
Annual stock price appreciation: –1.2% (historical average of 10-year negative rolling returns).
Annual dividend growth rate: 5%.
Necessary starting yield: 7.5%.

you should always buy or sell according to exact criteria. There is one situation, however, in which I do think selling right away makes sense.

So as with the earlier scenarios, I will give you some guidelines.

Say the money has been compounding for a number of years, and you're getting close to that 10-year mark or have surpassed it. Perhaps an emergency comes up where you need cash. If at all possible, find it somewhere else. Even if you have to borrow money, it might be worth it to avoid interrupting the compounding machine.

For example, you can get a home equity loan for 5% or even a credit card loan for 10%. If your dividend stocks are yielding 11% and generating 12% average annual returns (which are going to increase

Table 8.14   Bull Market with 5% Dividend Growth

	5 Years	10 Years	15 Years	20 Years
Yield (dividends not reinvested)	5.7%	7.3%	9.3%	11.9%
Annual income	$571	$729	$930	$1,187
Yield on cost (dividends reinvested)	$688	$1,040	$1,520	$2,159
Annual income	6.9%	10.4%	15.2%	21.6%
Average annual return	14.69%	14.19%	13.77%	13.4%
Total value	$19,840	$37,705	$69,242	$123,749

Assumptions:
Bull market, 5% dividend growth.
$10,000 investment.
Stock price appreciation: 10% (above historical average).
Dividend growth rate: 5%.
Necessary starting yield: 4.7%.

as the years go by), it might be worth it to borrow the money instead of dipping into your dividend stocks. As long as those stocks have a higher yield (after taxes) than the cost to borrow funds, keeping the compounding going might be a good idea.

You've already put in the hard work and waited years for the reward; make sure you get it.

At least once a year, look at your stocks to see if any of the following has occurred:

- Increased payout ratio
- Decline in cash flow, earnings, or sales
- Change in dividend policy

The Vulcan Materials Company example earlier in the chapter showed how keeping an eye on the payout ratio might have tipped you off that there was going to be a problem with the dividend.

If the company's payout ratio suddenly spikes, investigate why.

Same with a decrease in the company's sales, cash flow, or earnings. You want to have a clear understanding of why the numbers are falling and, importantly, how it affects the payout ratio. If the payout ratio is low enough, the falloff in cash flow may not threaten the company's ability to raise the dividend. However, if the company's financial performance could put the dividend hike in jeopardy, you want to know that before it happens.

If you see the payout ratio climbing quickly, or sales, cash flow, or earnings dropping, it doesn't mean you have to sell the stock right away. But at that point, I'd start looking at the company's performance every quarter rather than just once a year to see whether the situation is addressed and corrected.

If you see the problems continuing, I wouldn't wait too long to sell. At that point, you can take your capital and find another dividend-paying stock with better metrics.

A change in dividend policy may be a bit more serious. If the company cuts the dividend, sell.

A company with a history of raising dividends that suddenly cuts the dividend has made a profound statement. Management is clearly not confident in the company's future and ability to grow the dividend. Furthermore, the whole reason you're in the stock—to generate ever-increasing income—no longer exists.

If a company keeps the dividend the same instead of raising it, that's not quite as cut-and-dried. Each situation is a bit different. Not raising the dividend after 40 straight years of hikes is a more significant event than no dividend hike from a company with a seven-year track record of increases.

If you've been compounding for a while and have a great yield, you don't necessarily have to sell right away. See whether the company can get things going in the right direction again. Some companies have a tendency to start and stop dividend boosts. They might raise the dividend for five years, then keep it flat for three, raise it again for four, and so on.

Take a look at the transcripts of the company's conference call, and see whether management addresses why the dividend wasn't raised. If not, call investor relations and see what they say. As an owner of the company, you have every right to ask what's going on.

If you're enjoying an 11% yield and the company doesn't lift the dividend, but the payout ratio is reasonable and the company is still seeing growth in sales, earnings, and cash flow, there may not be a reason to panic.

In other words, take a good look at what's going on and use your judgment. With tools you now have, you can assess whether a company is healthy enough to continue to provide you with the income and returns that you expect. If it still can generate those returns, even though it did not raise the dividend, and if your yield is satisfactory, keep the stock. If, however, you have concerns that the dividend is not stable and may be cut, you're better off selling and looking for other opportunities.

Summary

- You can achieve an 11% yield and a 10-year average total return of 12% in 10 years.
- To do it, you need a 4.7% starting yield and 10% dividend growth, assuming the market performs as it has historically.
- Try to invest in stocks with a minimum of a 4% yield, 10% annual dividend growth, and a maximum payout ratio of 75%.
- Calculate the payout ratio based on cash flow from operations or free cash flow.

- You can make gobs of money reinvesting dividends in a stock that declines.
- Because I'm such a nice guy, I'm providing a free calculator at www.getrichwithdividends.com and www.wealthyretirement .com to help you figure out the future yields and total returns of your stock based on the variables that you enter.

CHAPTER 9

DRIPs and Direct Purchase Plans

I hope by now you see the wisdom of reinvesting dividends if you're attempting to build wealth for the long term.

Typically, the easiest way to do it is through your broker. Most brokers do not charge commissions or fees for reinvesting dividends. If yours does, find a new one. There's really no reason to pay a fee or commission on such a small transaction.

When you allow your broker to reinvest the dividends for you, all of your portfolio information is in one convenient place.

Not all brokers have the same options available. For example, Schwab and E*TRADE don't allow you to reinvest dividends of foreign stocks that trade on U.S. exchanges called American Depositary Receipts (ADRs). An example of an ADR would be drug giant Novartis (NYSE: NVS). The company is based in Switzerland but trades on the New York Stock Exchange

On the other hand, TD Ameritrade allows you to reinvest your dividends in ADRs.

In my opinion, this is a significant issue. A well-balanced portfolio will include companies located outside the United States. The inability to reinvest the dividends into the stock is a deal killer if you're trying to create wealth through dividend reinvestment.

Scottrade has a unique program called Flexible Reinvestment Program (FRIP). You can't automatically reinvest your dividends in the stock that pays them. Rather, the dividends can be reinvested in any eligible stock or exchange-traded fund (ETF), including those that don't pay dividends. The advantage is that the investor has more control over where to allocate the dividend. The disadvantage is that it requires more work for the investor and you can't buy fractional shares as you can with a traditional dividend reinvestment.

Scottrade's FRIP is an interesting idea, but what I like about dividend reinvestment plans (DRIPs) is how simple they are and that the investor doesn't have to think about it. As long as the investor is comfortable with the stock, she can set it and forget it.

Long-term investing success comes from investing in quality stocks and then doing a whole lot of nothing. Letting those dividends compound year after year is what will lead to building wealth. When the investor has more decisions to make, like in the FRIP program, it usually leads to worse outcomes.

Consider if you were invested in Intel. In October 2013, the stock was trading at around $22 and had a 4% dividend yield. Wall Street considered the chip maker a dinosaur, saying that the PC was dead and that Intel had not successfully grabbed market share in the mobile space.

If you had one of those flexible reinvestment programs and listened to Wall Street analysts, which you should never do, you might have put your dividends into a stock that seemed to have better prospects.

A year later Intel is up 50%, trading in the mid 30s. It turns out the PC was very much alive. Had you automatically reinvested your dividends in Intel, you would have picked up shares in the low 20s last year. Chances are, if you had to think about which stock to invest your dividends in, you would not have chosen Intel, considering how negative everyone was on the stock.

This is just another example of why we don't mind when a stock goes down or buying beaten-up stocks. As long as it's a quality company with enough cash flow to pay and raise the dividend, good things usually happen in the long term. You may have to put up with some pain and aggravation in the short term, but that lets you pick up more shares on the cheap.

Additionally, if we have another meltdown like we had in 2008 and early 2009, how many of us would have the guts to put the dividend payments right back into the market? Many people would think, "The market is tanking right now. I'll invest it later when stocks are lower." The only problem is I promise that those same people will not call the bottom. They'll wait until things look better, in which case the market will be considerably higher already.

Table 9.1   Brokers Offering Free DRIPs

Broker	Details
Schwab	Does not allow DRIPs of ADRs
E*TRADE	Does not allow DRIPs of ADRs
Fidelity	No restrictions
TD Ameritrade	No restrictions
Scottrade	Does not offer DRIPs, offers FRIP

By automatically reinvesting the dividends, they are guaranteed to put at least some money to work at or near the bottom of the market. Their own emotions of fear and greed, which ruin many investors, won't get in the way.

Table 9.1 shows you some of the major online discount brokers that do not charge for dividend reinvestment but have certain details you should know about.

However, not everyone likes to keep his or her stock in a brokerage account. Some prefer to deal directly with the company they're invested in.

Those people can usually reinvest their dividends through the company.

You can also buy more stock directly from the company if it offers a direct stock purchase plan (DSPP).

With a direct stock purchase plan, you send your check right to the company, and it credits your account with more shares. If you own 100 shares of a $20 stock and send the company another $200, your account will show that you are the proud owner of 110 shares (assuming there are no fees, which there often are—we'll get to that in a minute).

But here's why I don't like company DRIPs and DSPPs: They often have fees and commissions that are higher than those of a broker.

For example, let's take a look at Altria (NYSE: MO), a company that qualifies under the 10–11–12 System. Its yield is 4.7% and it has averaged over 11% dividend growth for the past 10 years.

Figure 9.1 shows the list of fees you would have to pay to reinvest your dividends or purchase stock directly from Altria.

Let's break down these fees. First it will cost you $10 to set up the plan. If you want to purchase stock directly, it will cost $5 plus $0.03 per share. If you buy more than 167 shares at any one time, the

Initial Setup Fee	$10.00
Cash Purchase Fee	$5.00
Ongoing Automatic Investment Fee	$2.50
Purchase Processing Fee (per share)	$0.03
Dividend Reinvestment Fee	5% of amount reinvested up to a maximum of $3.00
Batch Sale Fee	$15.00
Batch Sale Processing Fee (per share)	$0.12
Batch Maximum Sales Fee	N/A
Market Order Sale Fee	$25.00
Market Order Processing Fee (per share)	$0.12
Market Order Maximum Sales Fee	N/A

Figure 9.1   Fees When Reinvesting Dividends or Purchasing Stock Directly from Altria

Source: Computershare

cost likely will be more expensive than using a discount broker that normally charges $10 to buy stock.

You can see it will cost you a bunch of money to sell any of your shares—$25, plus $0.12 per share. That's a lot more than you'll pay at a discount broker. The only way this plan makes sense is if you're using a full-service broker that charges you more than you would pay in the direct purchase plan.

But what really steams my britches (Is that a saying? Sounds like it should be.) is that it will cost you as much as $3 to reinvest your dividends.

If you receive $100 in dividends, using the DRIP, you'll get to reinvest only $97 because Altria is charging you $3 each time you reinvest your dividends. That's money that belongs in your pocket. It's money that *will* stay in your pocket if you're using most brokers to reinvest the dividend.

Let's look at another company. (See Figure 9.2.) Clorox has similar fees to Altria for direct purchase. However, you won't pay anything to reinvest (other than the $15 initial setup fee).

In my mind, there is no reason to pay these fees. If investing or reinvesting directly is more convenient than using a broker, you'd

Initial Setup Fee	$15.00
Cash Purchase Fee	$5.00
Ongoing Automatic Investment Fee	$0.00
Purchase Processing Fee (per share)	$0.03
Dividend Reinvestment Fee	Company Paid
Batch Sale Fee	$15.00
Batch Sale Processing Fee (per share)	$0.12
Batch Maximum Sales Fee	N/A
Market Order Sale Fee	$25.00
Market Order Processing Fee (per share)	$0.12
Market Order Maximum Sales Fee	N/A

Figure 9.2 Clorox Plan Fee

Source: The Clorox Company

have to weigh the pros and the cons and decide whether the additional fees are worth the added convenience.

But for a portfolio of stocks, it actually is far less convenient to keep track of 5, 10, or 15 separate accounts rather than one brokerage account containing all of your stocks, where, by the way, you'll probably pay less out-of-pocket for all of your transactions.

The one wrinkle in all of this, where it may be worth your time to consider a DRIP, is when the company offers the stock at a discount.

You heard me right. There are some (not too many) companies that allow you to reinvest your dividends at a discount from the current market price. That's free money right there.

For example, water utility Aqua America (NYSE: WTR) offers a 5% discount when you reinvest your dividends.

As I write this, the stock is trading at $23.59. If you were to reinvest your dividends today, you'd pay $22.41 per share. Not too shabby. That's a built-in extra 5% on all shares that you buy through reinvested dividends over the lifetime of the account. Considering we're banking on a long-term average of only 7.84% annual gain in the stock to meet our goals, you're nearly already there with the portion of your money that's reinvested. (The shares bought with the original principal still need to gain their 7.84% per year.)

You've seen the power of compounding dividends. You understand that you want to buy stocks as cheaply as you can. Here's a way to do it for $0.95 on the dollar. The discount will help you accumulate more shares that will generate more dividends that will lead to more shares, and on and on.

Healthcare Realty Trust (NYSE: HR), a real estate investment trust specializing in health care, charges no fees or commissions for direct purchases or reinvestment of dividends and allows you to reinvest the dividend at a 5% discount.

Not many companies offer discounts to shareholders—only about 73 at the moment. If you're interested in a DRIP, be sure to visit the company's investor relations page on its website and closely examine all fees, commissions, discounts, and the like so that you have a clear understanding of what your costs will be versus keeping the stock with your broker.

As you can tell, I think the only time it makes sense to reinvest directly with the company is if you're getting a discount or if you're with a full-service broker that will charge you more than the company charges for each transaction. But even the full-service guys often allow you to reinvest your dividends for free, so look at all of the costs involved before making a decision.

Summary

- DRIPs and DSPPs can be a convenient way to reinvest dividends and buy more shares, but doing that often is easier through your broker, particularly if you own more than one stock.
- Not all brokers' dividend reinvestment options are the same. Get all the details from yours to make sure it fits your needs. In most cases, I recommend the most convenient and automatic method so that you don't have to make any decisions where emotion will get in the way.

- DRIPs and DSPPs often charge fees for setting up the plan, reinvesting dividends, and buying and selling shares, making it cheaper to use your discount broker.
- Some companies offer discounts of as much as 5% on reinvested dividends. In those cases, it may be worth participating in a DRIP—but be sure that other fees don't eliminate the benefit of the discount.
- Fifteen dollars to set up a DRIP? Are you kidding me?!

CHAPTER

10

Using Options to Turbocharge Your Returns

For many investors, options are scary. These investors have heard horror stories about people who got burned trading options, or that they're complicated, or that they're not for the little guy.

There are complex options strategies, and people do lose money when they speculate (there are also many investors who make money) with options. Most people who lose money trading options do so because they buy options. In a moment, I'm going to show you how to be the seller, the person who is more often on the winning side of the trade.

The strategy that I'm going to show you is simple, carries no risk to your principal (only opportunity risk), and can boost your returns by double digits annually.

First let's go over definitions of the two kinds of options: puts and calls.

> Put: A contract giving the buyer of the option the right, but not the obligation, to *sell* stock to the seller of the option at a specified price by a specified date.
>
> Call: A contract giving the buyer of the option the right, but not the obligation, to *buy* stock from the seller of the option at a specified price by a specified date.

Let's look at an example.

Shares of Microsoft are trading at $26. In July, an investor buys the January $30 call for $1. This means the call buyer has the right (but not the obligation) to demand the shares of Microsoft at $30 from the call seller at any time between now and the third Friday in January. (Options typically expire on the Saturday following the third Friday of the month. The third Friday of the month is the last day the options can be traded.) That $30 price is called the strike price—the price at which the seller of the call agrees to sell the stock to the buyer if demanded.

Why would someone want to enter into a contract to buy shares of Microsoft at $30 in the future if today he can buy them at $26? Because he thinks that by January, the stock is going to be higher than $30. Maybe he thinks it will be $35 by then, and to secure the right to buy it at $30, it will only cost $1.

If Microsoft is above $30 by January, the call buyer can demand the stock at $30, or he can sell the call at a profit. If the stock is trading at $35, he should be able to sell the call for at least $5, turning his $1 per share investment into $5.

Buying the call allows him to participate in Microsoft's upside while risking only $1 per share instead of $26. However, unlike owning Microsoft shares, the call option has an expiration date.

If the stock does not go above $30, the call expires worthless, and the seller of the call keeps the $1.

Puts act the same way, only the buyer of the put has the right (but not the obligation) to sell the stock at a certain price. If an investor owns Microsoft at $26, she may buy a $24 put to limit her losses.

If tomorrow it's discovered that Microsoft's code has been secretly stealing the personal information from every PC user in the world, the government shuts the company down, and the stock falls to zero, the buyer of the put can force the seller to buy her shares at $24.

Buying a put on a stock you own is like buying insurance. You hope to never need it but are glad you have it if you do. However, puts aren't right for everyone. If the price of a put costs 10% of the amount you invested in the stock, and the put expires in 6 months, you'll have to determine whether it's worth it to give up 10% to mitigate the risk.

If you want to learn all about options and strategies, there are tons of books on the subject, including *Get Rich with Options* by my friend and colleague Lee Lowell.

Covered Calls: The Espresso of Income Investing

Investing in dividend stocks is like a good strong cup of coffee for your portfolio. It puts some giddyap in your finances and helps you achieve your goals. Just like a cup of coffee gives you a jump start in the morning.

Some people need a little bit more help, particularly in the afternoon or maybe at night if they're going out. So rather than a cup of regular coffee, they kick it into overdrive and order an espresso.

A regular cup of coffee really doesn't do much for me. A shot of espresso, however, is like rocket fuel. I'm raring to go.

That's what a covered call is to your portfolio. It's like a shot of espresso to increase your returns.

> Covered call: When an investor owns shares of a company and sells a call option against those shares—agreeing to sell the shares at a predetermined price by a specified date at the call buyer's demand.

When an investor sells a covered call, he already owns the stock he is selling the call against, and agrees to sell the stock to the call buyer at the strike price (the specified price) by a certain date if the call buyer demands it.

So going back to our Microsoft example, if you own the stock at $26 and sell the January $30 (the strike price) call for $1 (per share), you will have to sell your stock to the call buyer for $30 by the third Friday in January if she exercises the contract (demands it).

Let's assume that it is July, so January is six months away. Let's look at some scenarios.

Best-case scenario. Microsoft stock trades up to $29.99 at expiration (third Friday in January). The call expires worthless and you keep the $1 per share. You've earned two dividend payments of $0.28 each for a total of $0.56. The stock is also up $3.99 since you bought it.

Worst-case scenario. It is discovered that Microsoft has been cooking its books for years, Bill Gates and the rest of the executives go to prison and the stock falls to zero. You'll at least get $1 out of the deal, as you'll keep the $1 from the now-worthless call. The call is worthless because no one is going to force you to sell a stock to him for $30, when the price of the stock is below $30.

The $1 helps protect the investor from some downside. And if you're a long-term investor, particularly if you're interested in the dividend or reinvesting the dividend, the stock's decline doesn't matter much to you. It matters only when you're ready to sell. In the meantime, if the stock slips to $23, you're still reinvesting the dividends at a lower price, and, oh, yeah, you get to keep the $1 per share, which is equivalent to another 3.8%.

Annoying scenario. Microsoft trades up to $33. Your call buyer can exercise her option forcing you to sell your shares to her for $30. Don't forget, you'll also keep the $1 she paid you, so it's like you're selling it for $31. Even though the stock is 7 points higher, you still made $5 ($4 profit plus $1 for the call) on a $26 stock in 6 months, or 19.2%, so it's not the end of the world.

But you did miss out on greater profits, which is the risk when you sell a call. Imagine if you made the same transaction, but instead, Apple bought Microsoft for $50 per share. You'd be a little more annoyed that you were missing out on all that extra profit.

As I've said repeatedly, there's no such thing as a free lunch on Wall Street. If you're going to make an easy $1 per share by selling a call, you're taking on the risk that you'll have to sell your stock at a lower price than where it might trade in the future.

That doesn't mean you'll suffer a loss, though. Let's be very clear about that. If you sell a call at a strike price that is higher than the price you paid for the stock, *you cannot suffer a loss as a result of the call being exercised.* That's an important concept to understand.

You can, of course, suffer a loss if the stock goes lower and you sell it. But selling a call with a strike price above what you paid for the stock cannot result in a loss to you, only a loss of opportunity if the stock goes higher than your strike price.

Options: Where 1 Equals 100

Option contracts are conducted in groups of 100 shares. If you sell one call, you are agreeing to sell 100 shares of stock. The $1 per share for selling the call would result in $100 cash being put into your account. If the option was exercised and you had to sell your shares at $30, you would receive $3,000 because you'd be getting paid $30 per share for 100 shares.

Even if the stock price is above the strike of the call you sold, you don't always have to sell your stock. If Microsoft is trading at $33 and you've sold the January $30 call, rather than selling your stock, you can buy back the call, albeit at a loss. So perhaps you'll have to pay $3.50 for the call that you sold for $1, incurring a loss of $2.50 per share. But you may determine that it's worth it if you own the stock, are reinvesting the dividends, and are building up a nest egg.

Or you may even be able to buy back the call at a profit. The values of options decay as the expiration date gets closer. If Microsoft is trading at $30.25 the day before expiration, you may be able to buy back the calls at $0.50, in which case you get to keep your stock and still make a $0.50 profit on the call that you originally sold for $1.

Option Prices

A few key variables affect option prices. They include how far away the stock is from the strike price, time, and volatility.

> In the money: A call option whose stock is above the strike price or a put option whose stock is below the strike price. A $30 call and a $40 put would be in the money if the stock is trading at $35.
>
> At the money: An option whose stock is at the strike price. A $35 call and $35 put would be at the money if the stock is trading at $35.
>
> Out of the money: A call option whose stock is below the strike price or a put option whose stock is above the strike price. A $40 call and $30 put would be out of the money if the stock is trading at $35.

An in-the-money call option is a call whose strike price is below the current stock price.

Example: Freeport-McMoRan (NYSE: FCX) is trading at $37. A January $35 call is *in the money* because the strike price ($35) is below the current price ($37). The option is currently trading at $8. That's because the stock is already $2 in the money. The call has to be worth at least $2, because that's the profit an owner of the stock could make automatically upon purchase of the stock at $35. The remaining $6 is because of volatility, which we'll talk about in a moment.

If you were to sell the January $37 call, it would be *at the money*, because the current price and the strike price are the same. That call goes for $7, all of which is because of volatility. Someone who exercised the option and bought the stock at $37 would not have a gain or loss with the stock trading at the same price.

The January $40 call is *out of the money* because the $40 strike is above the current price of $37. The $40 strike will cost you $5.75, again all of which is because of volatility.

So now let's talk about volatility.

Volatility: An Option Seller's Best Friend

If you sell calls against your stocks, forget the family dog; volatility is your best friend. Volatility is a measure of how much the price of a stock fluctuates. The more the stock price bounces around, the more likely an option's strike price will be met, which is why stocks that are more volatile have higher-priced options.

Think of it this way: If you are buying an option that has very little chance of actually hitting the strike price, you probably won't be willing to pay very much for it. But if a stock is up three points one day, down six the next, up five the following day, and so on, there's a better chance your option will hit the strike price and become profitable. Because of the better odds, you will have to pay a higher price.

There have been many studies on volatility, and you can read all about it in various books about options. But I wanted to give you a simple explanation.

Transocean Limited (NYSE: RIG) happens to be a very volatile stock because it tends to react to price swings in oil. Another stock, such as B&G Foods (NYSE: BGS), might be in a similar price range, but its options are much cheaper because the stock isn't as volatile.

When you sell calls on volatile stocks, you collect a bigger payment from the buyer. The fact that it's more volatile increases the chance that your call could be exercised and you'll have to surrender your stock, but you're getting paid well to take that risk.

For example, if you bought Transocean at $21 and in late November 2014 sold the January 2016 $25 calls for $2.00, you'd make 9.5% on your money just from the calls alone ($2.00 divided by $21). If you owned the stock for a year while you're waiting for expiration of the call, you'd get paid another $3 in dividends (Transocean has an exceptionally high dividend), increasing your return to 23.8%. Finally, if the stock is above $25 and gets called away from you, you'd make 42.9% in 1 year.

Of course, the risk is that the stock is trading at $40 and you have to sell it for $25. But the fact that you made $3.00 in dividends plus $2.00 from the call, can take away some of the pain of the missed opportunity.

Plus, if the stock goes against you and falls to $20, you're still in the black because you collected the $2.00 from the call and the $3.00 in dividends. The call essentially lowers your break-even price from $21 to $18.

Time Is on Your Side

Time is the other component in an option's price. The longer the amount of time until expiration, the more the option will be worth. It makes sense. After all, the further away expiration is, the more time the stock has to hit the strike price. A stock with an option that expires in just a few weeks may have little chance of hitting an out-of-the-money strike price. Therefore, it would be very inexpensive.

Option prices decay with time. If a stock never moved a penny from the time you sold an option on it, you would see the option price slowly fall with the passage of time. As the expiration date gets closer, the price decline picks up momentum.

That's why I say time is on your side as a call seller. If you sell a call for a nice price, eventually the time component of the price will deteriorate. The option price could go higher if the stock gets more volatile or if the stock price climbs, but the time element will dwindle to zero like the sand in an hourglass.

In fact, it's possible you could sell an out-of-the-money call, see the stock rise to go in the money, and still make a profit.

Here's how.

In our Transcoean example, with the stock trading at $21 in November 2014, you sell the January 2016 $25 call for $2.00. In late December 2015, the stock is trading at $26. Because so much time has expired over the life of the option contract, there is very little time value left. So the January $25 call, which you sold for $2.00, may now be trading at $1.50, even though the stock is $1 in the money.

You could buy back the call for a profit of $0.50 ($2.00 − $1.50) and hang on to your stock, which is now trading at $26.

Who Should Sell Covered Calls?

Because the seller of the covered call may have to give up his stock, this strategy is more appropriate for investors who are seeking current income as opposed to those who are trying to build wealth via dividend reinvestment.

If you're trying to build a nest egg with a time horizon of 10 years, by reinvesting dividends, chances are that within those 10 years, we'll hit a bull market, stocks will rise, and any stock you sold covered calls against will be called away from you, disrupting the compounding dividend machine.

Of course, you could always take the money from the sale of the stock and put it into another dividend payer. But one of the appealing aspects of the dividend reinvestment method is how easy it is and how little time you have to devote to it.

Also, there is no way of automatically reinvesting the money you receive from selling the calls back into the stock. That's not a huge problem, but buying more stock with the money you receive from the calls is another step you'd have to take if you were trying to build up your holdings in that particular stock.

If you're selling covered calls against your position, you definitely want to be on top of it.

But the time commitment can certainly be worth it. If you're looking for current income, this is a terrific strategy to boost your returns. As you saw in the Transocean example, if the stock gets called away from you at $25, you'd have earned 42.9% instead of 33.3% from the dividends and price appreciation. If you weren't forced to sell the stock, you'd have earned an *extra* nearly 10% on a stock you were planning on hanging on to anyway to receive the dividend.

And if the stock gets called away from you, just take your gains and move on to the next dividend stock.

The only real downside is when the stock flies way past the strike price. That can be frustrating as you miss out on those additional profits. And chances are if you sell enough covered calls, it will happen to you. But over the long haul, it's worth putting in the extra time to manage your positions to get those extra double-digit returns year in and year out on your stocks.

Now, what happens if your stock takes a dive and you want to dump it but you sold a call against it? No problem, you just buy the call back, usually much cheaper. If Transocean falls to $18, your $25 call will likely fall right along with it. The decline of the call won't match that of the stock dollar for dollar, because, remember, an option's price is also made up of time and volatility components. But it should be lower, and you can buy back the call at a profit and then sell your stock.

For example, if you sell the Transocean $25 calls for $2.00 and the stock drops to $18, the option may be trading at $0.75. You'd buy it back and profit $1.25 ($2.00 – $0.75). The $1.25 profit on the calls offset some of the $3 loss on the stock.

Espresso isn't for everyone. Some people get jittery from all that caffeine. But others love the extra lift it provides. Covered calls are similar. Some investors don't want to commit the extra time to studying and managing their options positions. But for those who do, the extra boost to their portfolio's returns can be grande (sorry, I couldn't resist).

20% Annual Returns

There are various strategies for selling covered calls. Some investors like to sell out-of-the-money calls, accepting less premium for their calls to decrease the chances that the stock will be called away.

Others will sell in-the-money calls so that they maximize the income they collect from the calls and don't care if the stock is called away, even at a loss because the higher option premium will make up for it. This can also be an effective strategy in a bear market because if the stock falls, you may still keep your stock and you've collected the higher option premium.

Both of those strategies are effective, and the choice simply depends on what your priorities are in using covered calls and your market outlook. I tend to go right in the middle of those two strategies.

The method that I most often use and recommend is short term in nature and uses at-the-money or slightly out-of-the-money calls.

If I'm selling a covered call, I'm renting the stock, not buying to own. In other words, I don't care if the stock is called away from me. In fact, all the stock is to me is a vehicle for producing income. It's not something I'm planning to own for the long term. I don't care how good or bad management is, whether the company generates plenty of cash flow, or whether margins are increasing.

It is simply a three- or four-letter ticker symbol that will generate enough income for me to reach my goals.

What are my goals? I'm glad you asked. When selling covered calls, I'm trying to achieve 20% annualized returns.

If I can achieve a 3% or more return in 6 weeks, annualized that comes out to 26%. To achieve the 3% return, I need a combination of a dividend payment and option premium. If I make a little bit on the stock, that's just gravy.

Here's what I mean.

Let's say in the middle of September, International Paper (NYSE: IP) is trading at $48.25. The November $49 call can be sold for $1.30. The stock pays a $0.35 per share dividend in mid-November.

I buy International Paper for $48.25 and sell the November $49 call for $1.30. Before expiration I collect the $0.35 dividend. At expiration, one of three scenarios will have occurred:

- The stock is above our strike price of $49.
- The stock is at our strike price of $49.
- The stock is below our strike price of $49.

Let's look at the first scenario—the stock is above our strike price of $49.

November rolls around and International Paper shares have been strong. It's the third Friday in November (the last day you can trade an option before expiration) and International Paper is trading at $52.

If you do nothing, the stock will be called away from you, meaning you'll have to sell it at the agreed-upon price (strike price) of $49. You would keep the $1.30 option premium, the $0.35 dividend and the $0.75 capital gain (you bought the stock at $48.25 and sold it at $49 for a $0.75 gain). In total, you made $2.40 on the covered call or 5% ($2.40/48.25 = 0.05).

You may think 5% is nothing special, but remember, you made that in two months. Considering the average return on the stock market is about 8% for the entire year, 5% in 2 months is pretty strong. Annualized that 5% turns into 30% (12 months divided by 2 months equals 6. $6 \times 5\% = 30\%$).

If you decide you'd rather keep the stock because you think it's going higher, you could buy back the option so that your stock isn't called away from you. Because the stock is $3 higher than the strike price, you may pay $3.10 for the option.

In that case, you lost $1.80 on the option (sold it for $1.30 and bought it for $3.10) and made $0.35 on the dividend. You now have a $3.75 open gain on the stock, which you can sell at a later date, hopefully for a larger gain.

When the stock is right at the strike price or when the stock is below the strike price, your option will expire worthless. Technically, the buyer of the call can call your stock away; however, if it were trading right at $49, the call buyer would likely be better off just buying the stock in the open market. Commissions are usually higher for calling away a stock or having a stock called away versus buying or selling in the open market.

So if the call expires worthless, as the seller, you keep the premium and the stock.

Keep in mind that if the stock drops significantly, you can still be down a meaningful amount. If International Paper drops to $40 per share, yes, you still keep the $1.30 option premium for selling the call and the $0.35 dividend, but you're down $8.25 on the stock. If the stock falls hard and it isn't a long-term holding, at some point, you may decide to sell the stock for a loss and buy back the call at a gain.

If the stock drops to $40, the option will be essentially worthless because no one will buy your stock from you at $49 if it's trading at $40; you'll be able to buy back the call, perhaps for as little as $0.05.

If the stock were trading at $47 and there were still several weeks to go before expiration, you might be able to buy back the call at $0.50, making $0.80 on the option, but still be down $1.25 on paper.

When selling covered calls, I try to capture that 3% to 5% in 6 to 8 weeks. If I can generate those kinds of returns each trade and make those trades throughout the year, I should have no problem earning 20% on my money.

Of course, the market and the stocks have to cooperate. If there is a big correction or downturn in the market, it won't be as easy. On the other hand, selling a covered call on a quality dividend payer is a way to generate some extra income during a slide in the market.

The strategy for doing this is to sell at-the-money or slightly out-of-the-money calls on stocks whose ex-dividend dates are before the option expiration.

In the International Paper example, the stock's ex-dividend date was in mid-November and we sold a November call, which expired about a week after the stock's ex-dividend date.

That allows us to capture both the dividend and option premium if everything goes according to plan. But sometimes plans don't work the way you expect.

If the stock is above the strike price before the ex-dividend date, the call buyer might call the stock away from you to receive the dividend.

So if International Paper is trading at $52 in mid-November, the call buyer might exercise the option and call the stock away from you at $49. He buys the stock below the current market price *and* will be entitled to the dividend because he now owns it before the ex-dividend date.

As the option seller, you keep the full $1.30 option premium and sell the stock for $49, pocketing $0.75 per share. In total, you'd make $2.05 or 4.2% in less than 2 months—which still comes out to well over 20% annualized.

If over the course of the year, you made this trade over and over again, never being able to capture the dividend—just the option premium and the small gain on the stock, you'd still make more than 20% on your money.

Investors who use covered calls can also sell calls several months or even years out to get more option premium. In addition, they can sell calls that have a strike price that is much lower than the current price (deep in-the-money calls), for which they will receive more premium or much higher than the current price. In the latter case, they'll receive much less option premium but can capture more gains on the stock if it goes up.

Selling covered calls is a great way to generate short-term income, and you can do it in most individual retirement accounts. The risk, like with any stock, is that the stock goes down. You still get to keep the option premium and dividends, but there is still stock market risk. There is also opportunity risk in that you won't get to participate in endless upside on the stock. The gains are limited by the strike price.

But that's okay, because we're not entering this type of trade to try to hit a home run on the stock. We're trying to generate extra income.

Selling Puts

Some investors are big fans of selling naked puts. Unlike an out-of-the-money covered call in which you already own the security and you can't lose any money unless the stock price goes down, selling a naked put involves significant risk. The strategy is called *naked* because the option is not married to a stock. If you were short the stock and sold the put, it would not be naked.

When you sell a put, the buyer has the right to sell you the stock at the strike price before or at expiration. Therefore, when you sell a put, you need to be prepared to buy the stock.

Put sellers typically sell out-of-the-money puts—a strike price below the current market price.

In return, you receive the cash that the buyer pays for the put. If the stock does not reach the put's strike price, you keep the cash. If the put does wind up in the money, you may be forced to buy the stock, which can get expensive.

Think of it this way; the put buyer is purchasing insurance on her stock. If the stock price goes down, she is protected by the puts. You, as the put seller, are the insurance company. You collect and keep the insurance premium and take on the risk if something goes wrong.

Let's say Merck (NYSE: MRK) is trading at $60, and you sell 5 puts on Merck with a strike price of $55 for $1 per contract. Since option contracts represent 100 shares, you'll receive $100 per contract, or $500. If the Merck puts are in the money (below $55) and you are required to buy the stock, you will need to pay $27,750 (500 shares × $55 per share).

Investors who sell naked puts should do so *only* if they want to own the underlying stock at the strike price where the puts are sold. They also need to have the money available to purchase the stock if it is put (sold) to them.

Put sellers love this strategy because, in a bull market, it's like free money. They collect the cash from selling the puts and are not required to own any stock. (However, they don't participate in any upside if the stock goes higher.) If the stock slides, they not only keep the cash but also buy shares at a lower price than they would have earlier.

Using our Merck example, if Merck is trading at $60, an investor sells the puts with a $55 strike, and the stock is put to him at $55, the net cost will be $54. Don't forget, he received the $1 per share for selling the put. When Merck was trading at $60, if the investor would have been happy to own the stock at $54, the trade might be attractive.

The risk is that Merck could be sharply lower by the time the option expires. If one of Merck's drugs is shown to have nasty side effects and the stock slides to $50, the put seller is still on the hook to buy it at $55. Like the covered call, you can always buy the put back at a loss if the trade goes against you—before the stock is put to you.

A put-selling strategy is appealing to dividend investors who see a stock they want to buy but feel it's overpriced. They can sell the put and essentially be paid to wait to see if the stock price comes down. If it does, the investor can get the price she wants. If not, at least she collected some income during the process.

This can be an effective way of ensuring that you're buying low. When stock prices are rising and valuations are increasing, the put seller does not buy stock, but simply collects cash from the option premium. Then, when there is a correction or the stock falls, he is right there to scoop it up on the cheap.

Considering most investors put money to work at the wrong time—after the markets have gone considerably higher and take money out when markets fall, this is an effective strategy to ensure you're investing at the right time—when prices are low—and getting paid to wait until the time is right.

The risk comes from the possibility that you buy a stock much higher than it's currently worth.

In our Merck example, if the company reports a horrendous quarter and announces it has to pull its biggest-selling drug off the market because it turned out that instead of curing people, it was killing them, the stock might drop to $25. The put seller now owns a $25 stock at $55, where he was forced to buy it.

While I like put selling, it's more complicated than selling covered calls. For most investors, the covered call strategy is a better one for a very important reason: The risk is lower. The last thing you want to do when you're conservatively investing for income and for the future is to get blown up by an options trade.

When you write covered calls, other than your stock going down (which could happen regardless of selling calls), the worst that could happen is that your stock takes off and you're forced to sell it and miss out on some upside, or you sell the calls at a loss to keep the gains in the stock.

Summary

- Selling a covered call is a great way to boost the income you receive from your stock holdings.
- When you sell a covered call, it gives the buyer the right, but not the obligation, to buy your stock from you at a specified price (strike price) by a certain date (expiration date).
- When you sell an out-of-the-money covered call, your only risk is opportunity risk (although you can choose to buy the call back at a loss if you don't want to give up your stock).
- You need to actively monitor your covered call positions. A covered call strategy requires more attention by you, so you're no longer snoozing your way to wealth.
- Selling out-of-the-money, naked puts allows you to get paid to wait and see whether a stock you're interested in comes down in price, but it carries more risk than covered calls.
- Coffee doesn't do a thing for me. Espresso, however, turns me into Jim Carrey on uppers.

CHAPTER

11

Foreign Stocks

Some dividend payers, particularly in emerging markets, can offer very attractive yields, especially in comparison to their American counterparts.

In late 2011, while quality American companies were trading with yields around 3% to 4%, many emerging market and beaten-up European equities were paying double those yields. By late 2014, many of those high-yielding European and emerging market yields have dropped to be closer to their American counterparts.

Again, it's important to remember that Wall Street doesn't just give money away. Two equal stocks will not pay dividend yields that are so wide apart that one will be one and a half to twice that of its peer.

If company A is paying a yield of 7% and company B is paying 3.5%, it's because company A is riskier or Wall Street believes it's riskier. Great investors make lots of money when they can identify those companies that are mispriced because Wall Street is mistakenly scared of a stock or underestimated its performance.

The same is true when it comes to dividend yields. You'll want to find those companies whose yields are high compared to similar American companies because the Street has mispriced the stock.

But it is very important to realize that the higher yield typically involves higher risk. It doesn't mean you shouldn't take that risk, but you definitely need to be aware of it.

One Lump or Two?

Wall Street analysts have their own language. They say things like "Can you give some more granularity on that?" when they're asking a CEO for more details on a topic, or they might ask for more *color* on the quarter.

One of my favorite terms is *lumpy*. It means inconsistent. A company's profits might be described as lumpy if 1 quarter has earnings of $1 per share, the next has only $0.20 in earnings, and the following quarter it is $1.05. Sometimes that's because of a sales cycle or simply when a big contract gets signed, paid, or recognized.

I've extended *lumpiness* to dividend payments as well. Foreign stocks often have lumpy dividends. They might pay $1.65 per share in year 1, $1.32 in year 2, $1.77 in year 3, and $1.41 in year 4.

American companies typically try not to have the dividend flying all over the place like that. They do their best to keep the dividend consistent. If management is concerned that it might have to cut the dividend in the future, chances are it won't raise the dividend the year before so that the change doesn't appear to be a reduction in the dividend.

When it comes to companies located overseas, particularly in emerging markets, the dividends can vary widely from year to year. Currency fluctuation can play a big part in that. In the local currency, a company may pay a consistent dividend. But if that currency moves 10% per year against the dollar, an investor in the American depositary receipt (ADR) may get $2 per share in dividends one year and $1.80 the next year, all while the company actually shelled out the same amount in its local currency.

American depositary receipt (ADR): An instrument that trades on a U.S. exchange that represents shares (often one share) of a foreign stock. The ADR is denominated in U.S. dollars while the actual foreign stock is priced in the currency of the exchange where it trades. An owner of an ADR has the right to convert the ADR into shares of the foreign stock, although few people actually do.

For example, Chilean bank CorpBanca SA (NYSE: BCA) paid out dividends of Ch$51 billion (Ch$ = Chilean peso) in 2008, Ch$56 billion in 2009, and Ch$85 billion in 2010. An investor in Chile would

Table 11.1   CorpBanca Dividend History

	2008	2009	2010
Total dividends paid	Ch$51 billion	Ch$56 billion	Ch$86 billion
Dividends paid per share	Ch$0.22	Ch$0.25	$Ch0.37
Dividends paid per ADR	$0.61	$0.49	$0.86

Source: CorpBanca SA & Morningstar

have received Ch$0.22 per share in 2008, Ch$0.25 in 2009, and Ch$0.37 in 2010.

However, because the peso appreciated in 2009 from where it was for most of 2008, U.S. investors actually saw their dividend fall to $0.49 per ADR from $0.61. In 2010, when the peso fell, U.S. holders of the ADR received $0.86.

As you can see in Table 11.1, in 2009, CorpBanca actually paid more in total dividends and more per share in dividends, yet investors in the ADR received less per unit because of the currency appreciation.

This is an important concept to understand because it affects your dividends. Let's make up an example that will be easy to grasp.

The only currency accepted in Marc Lichtenfeld's Authentic Italian Trattoria is the Lichtenfeldian dollar (L$). At the time I take my company public and sell stock, the L$ is trading at parity with the U.S. dollar: L$1 = $1. The stock is also denominated in Lichtenfeldian dollars.

Let's assume that one ADR represents one share of stock.

I declare a dividend of L$1 per share. Because the Lichtenfeldian dollar (also known as the Lichty) is trading at a 1:1 ratio with the U.S. dollar, ADR holders will receive $1 per share.

The following year, because of the success of my baked ziti, the Lichtenfeldian dollar appreciates to L$2 for every $1.

I continue to pay $L1 per share in dividends. However, because the Lichty is now worth $2, ADR holders will receive only $0.50.

In year 3, after a food reviewer gets a nasty case of the heaves following a bad batch of clams casino, the Lichty plummets to $L0.50 for every $1. Now $1 is worth L$2. I continue to pay a dividend of L$1 per share, but now that equals $2.

So, over the course of three years, I paid out L$1 per share in each year, yet the holders of the ADR saw their distribution fluctuate between $2 and $0.50 because of the currency swings.

Lumpy Perpetual Dividend Raisers?

This lumpiness in dividends ADR holders receive makes it difficult to find foreign Perpetual Dividend Raisers.

Dividend programs usually are carefully managed. When earnings and cash flow are somewhat predictable, executives will have a strategy for how they will distribute dividends and whether there will be a growth plan. If there is enough excess cash to grow the dividend each year, usually there will be a target growth rate.

Even if a foreign management team has that kind of dividend strategy in place, what ADR holders will receive is out of their control because of the movement of currency prices.

A company could raise its dividend 5% in a year, but if the currency appreciates against the dollar, ADR holders could see a lower payout, even with the rise in the dividend.

Therefore, often it is very difficult to find foreign companies that qualify as Perpetual Dividend Raisers. Not only does the company have to cooperate, but the currency market has to as well. And the chances of the dollar steadily increasing over another currency year after year are small.

This is not a political or economic argument. It's not that I'm bearish on the dollar or the United States. It's just that markets, particularly currency markets, seldom move in one direction. Over many years, there might be a trend. The dollar may appreciate over a particular currency over 5 or 10 years. But that move is highly unlikely to be a straight line.

And that fluctuation could affect a company's ability to be called a Perpetual Dividend Raiser. If the dollar does in fact appreciate and the company is raising dividends, it could turn out to be a nice investment over the years. However, it will be far less predictable than other types of stocks that we've been talking about in this book.

If you want to be assured that you're getting a greater income stream year after year, a foreign dividend payer might not get the job done.

Another issue when it comes to foreign dividend payers is the frequency of the dividend payments. Investors in American companies are used to receiving a quarterly dividend. Foreign companies often pay only once or twice a year.

For investors who rely on dividend income, that means just one or two big checks coming in rather than four smaller ones.

It's not a big deal for investors who don't rely on the income every quarter, but for those who do, the timing can be a problem. Even for investors who are reinvesting the dividend, the once-a-year payment can affect total return negatively.

When you reinvest a dividend that you receive four times a year, you're spacing your investment out over four periods at four different prices. It's very similar to dollar cost averaging, where money is invested over periods of time.

If you're receiving only one payment a year, all of that money is going back into the stock at once. If the stock runs up in anticipation of the dividend, you end up reinvesting the entire year's dividend at a high price.

This is not unusual because of something called dividend capture.

Dividend capture: Buying a stock just before its ex-dividend date (the date on which a new investor is not entitled to the most recent dividend) to capture the dividend and then selling the stock shortly afterward.

When investors engage in a dividend capture strategy, the idea is to own the stock just long enough to be paid the dividend. Then they move on to the next stock.

Stocks that pay a high level of dividends are particularly attractive to users of the dividend capture strategy. A stock that pays a large dividend only once per year would definitely be on their radar.

This is important because if enough buyers are interested in getting in right before the dividend is paid (whether they're dividend capture investors or they plan on being legitimate, long-term holders), the stock price will advance as more buyers come into the stock.

That's a problem for the investor who is reinvesting dividends once per year. If the stock runs higher every time long-term investors are going to reinvest their dividends, their returns are going to be far lower than returns on a stock that isn't attracting this attention right before the dividend is paid.

The dividend capture strategy isn't directed just at foreign stocks. It can and does happen to American companies as well. But with four periods throughout the year and the fact that the dividend is broken up into four pieces, the likelihood of being severely affected is lower than if you're invested in a stock that pays out a 6% dividend once a year.

Other Risks

When you invest in a company that is located and trading in another country, you take on additional risks, such as political, economic, and regulatory.

Although American regulators and auditors are by no means perfect, as investors who lost money in Enron or with Bernie Madoff will attest, the system does offer a reasonable amount of assurance that reported financial results are legitimate. Someone who is sharp and committed to defrauding investors will likely succeed, but that is by far the exception, not the rule.

In some other countries, investors generally do not know how good the regulators and auditors are. As an average investor, you may do your due diligence on a Chilean telecom company, but, in truth, you have no idea how thorough regulators and auditors are in Chile. They may be terrific—the best in the world, for all you know. But that's the point. You *don't* know.

So, when a foreign company reports financial results, there has to be a certain level of trust—even more so than with an American company, especially if the country we're talking about is an emerging market.

You might think that's ethnocentric to say, but it's the truth. Countries with long-standing stock markets, such as England and Australia, generally have solid accounting practices and rules. On the other side are countries like China, which are notorious for hosting shell corporations and companies that cook the books.

If that's not scary enough, in certain countries you run the risk of political or economic upheaval. As I write this, Argentina is going through a very high level of inflation and has been for years. Although the rate is being reported officially as around 15%, most people say it's really above 40%.

As a result, Argentina may eventually (or by the time you read this may already have) devalue its currency, which will hurt its businesses and their ability to pay dividends.

Some countries could have political upheaval, which may impact a company's ability to grow profits and dividends. Maybe the turmoil sinks the share price of a great company, allowing you to buy more shares cheaply, before it eventually comes back in favor. Or perhaps it never comes back because the new leader of the country is corrupt, antibusiness, whatever.

In 2014, as Russia endured economic sanctions because of its military action in Ukraine, Russia's parliament passed a law that prohibited any major Russian media company from being more than 20% owned by investors outside of Russia.

That was a problem for CTC Media (Nasdaq: CTCM), a Russian television broadcaster that trades on the Nasdaq, which is incorporated in Delaware and paid a 7% yield before the passage of the law.

The stock was attractive to some investors because of the strong yield and the fact that the company reported its results in U.S. dollars.

However, once the law was passed, the stock lost nearly 50% of its value in just a few weeks. Nothing had changed regarding its actual business. Its inventory of ads was still pretty much sold out. Advertisers weren't pulling their business. But because of the political climate, the stock was hit hard.

That's a perfect example of how foreign governments can often be a wild card when investing outside the United States.

Now that I've probably scared you out of investing in anything other than the bluest American blue chips, let me tell you why foreign stocks are a good addition to your portfolio.

Because of all of those extra risk factors mentioned above, you're often compensated for that risk in the form of a higher dividend yield. As I explained earlier, a solid dividend in the United States right now is 3% to 4%. In emerging markets, you can find high-quality companies paying 5% to 6%.

If you're invested in the right company in the right market, you can obtain high yields with significant capital gains as well.

Any financial advisor worth his khakis will tell you to diversify your portfolio. You should have small caps, large caps, mid caps, American companies, and international companies, including those in emerging markets.

A portfolio of dividend stocks is no different. Although there are some additional risks, you also take extra risk by not diversifying.

For example, in 2008, the S&P 500 fell 37%. Anyone who was invested in the Tunisian stock market (and who wasn't?) saw a gain of 10%.

That's obviously an extreme example, but it illustrates the point that investing in other markets can produce gains when the rest of your portfolio is going down.

You need to do your homework when investing in a foreign dividend payer and be sure you understand the additional and unique risks for that particular stock in that particular country. But if you are aware of the risks and the market is adequately compensating you for them, they can be an important part of your portfolio. I would just caution that you don't chase yield and overweight your portfolio with these kinds of stocks.

Treat these stocks like dessert. As we tell our kids, ice cream is a sometimes food. Most of what they eat consists of vegetables, protein, fruit, and grains. And then sometimes they get ice cream. Your dividend portfolio should consist mostly of Perpetual Dividend Raisers that can qualify for the 10–11–12 System. But it's perfectly fine— in fact, it's recommended—to have a sprinkling of foreign dividend payers in there, as long as you're aware that they will not likely be Perpetual Dividend Raisers. But that extra yield you get may make it worth your while.

Summary

- Many foreign dividend payers currently have considerably higher yields than their American counterparts.
- Foreign companies are usually not classified as Perpetual Dividend Raisers because of currency fluctuation.
- The higher yields are compensation for higher political and economic risk.
- Many foreign dividends are paid only once or twice a year.
- You should have been invested in the Tunisian stock market in 2008. Duh!

CHAPTER

12

Taxes

I was hesitant to write this chapter. In fact, I didn't even include it in the table of contents in the proposal to my publisher. I despise how complicated taxes can be. It's why this chapter wasn't in my original plans for the book. However, taxes are an important issue that needs to be addressed.

Keep in mind that I am not a tax expert. I will cover only the basics of tax law as it pertains to dividends. If you have any questions, you should *always* seek the advice of a tax professional.

Here's what you need to know:

Dividend tax rate = 15%

That's it. Any questions?

Okay, it's a little more complex than that.

In 2014, most Americans will pay 15% on dividends held in taxable accounts. Note, if your dividends are in a tax-deferred account, like a 401(k) or an individual retirement account (IRA), you will not pay taxes on the dividends for the year in which they were received. You may pay taxes on them when you withdraw the funds in the future.

That's been the case since 2003, when President Bush signed the Jobs and Growth Tax Reconciliation Relief Act. In 2010, President Obama extended the tax cuts that set the dividend tax rate at 15%.

If the tax cuts expire, it is expected that dividends will be taxed at the individual's ordinary income tax rate. Of course, in politics, anything can happen, and tax policy may change considerably by the time you read this.

But if you're reading this just when it was published because you ran to the bookstore or ordered it online as soon as the book was available (thanks, Uncle Bob), you will probably pay 15% tax on your qualified dividends.

There are exceptions.

If you are in the 10% or 15% tax bracket—your taxable income is less than $36,900 as an individual or $73,800 filing jointly—you will not pay taxes on your dividends. That is a huge advantage as you not only can collect income tax free but also can reinvest those dividends and not worry about having to come up with the cash on April 15 to pay taxes on those dividends.

Of course, if you stick with the 10–11–12 System long enough, your dividend income could push you into another tax bracket, which may mean that you'll have to pay the 15% or whatever the rate is when the income is high enough to change your bracket.

It would be a good problem to have but one you should keep your eye on, and if you're not already, consider working with a tax professional as your income gets close to or climbs above the limit for the 15% tax bracket.

Those in the highest 39.6% bracket, whose taxable income is $406,750 filing individually or $457,600 filing jointly, will pay 20% on their dividends, plus another 3.6% that goes toward paying for the Affordable Care Act.

Foreign Taxes

It's bad enough you have to pay U.S. taxes; now you're being asked to pay taxes in other countries? Well, yes and no. But don't worry; you're not getting taxed twice.

Depending on the tax laws of the country where the company is based, taxes may already be taken out by the time you receive the dividend.

For example, if you are paid a dividend on shares of Telefónica (NYSE: TEF), the Spanish mobile phone company, the government of Spain will help itself to 21% of your dividend payment.

When you calculate your U.S. taxes, you fill out Internal Revenue Service (IRS) Form 1116, which will generate a tax credit on the amount paid to a foreign government.

To be clear, you don't get the money back; you just won't owe taxes on the dividends to the U.S. IRS.

Paying taxes to a foreign government is a pretty regular occurrence. If you've ever owned a mutual fund that owns foreign stocks, chances are you've paid foreign taxes and had to claim the foreign tax credit before.

Some countries, like Argentina, don't tax you at all, in which case, you'll just pay the U.S. tax rate. But you're going to pay someone. Uncle Sam, Uncle Jacques, or Uncle Pedro is going to get his money. You can be sure of that.

There also can be different rules depending on the type of account you hold your stock in. For example, if you own foreign stocks inside an IRA, *you are not eligible for a tax credit.*

This is an important concept to understand if you are investing in a foreign stock in a tax-deferred account whose country withholds taxes on your dividends.

You'll still pay foreign taxes on that dividend and *not get it back if it's in your IRA or 401(k).*

For example, if you owned French oil company Total SA (NYSE: TOT) in your IRA, 30% of your dividends would be withheld by the French government. Because the stock is in your tax-deferred retirement account, you would not be eligible for the U.S. tax credit.

If you owned Total in your taxable account, you'd still pay the 30% withholding, but then the IRS would give you a tax credit for the same amount.

Canada is the exception and will reduce the withholding to zero for investments held in U.S. retirement accounts.

Additionally, your adjusted gross income may affect the amount of the foreign tax credit that you are eligible for. Be sure to talk to a tax adviser with any questions.

Tax-Deferred Strategies

In Chapter 6, I mentioned real estate investment trusts (REITs), master limited partnerships (MLPs), business development companies (BDCs), and closed-end funds, which often classify a significant portion or all of their distributions to shareholders as returns of capital.

As we discussed, a return of capital typically is not taxed in the year in which the distribution is received. Instead, it lowers the cost basis on the stock, and you will pay capital gains on the adjusted cost basis when you sell the stock.

How Return of Capital Works	
Purchase stock:	$10
Return of capital:	$1
Adjusted cost basis:	$9
Sell stock:	$20
Capital gain:	$11

In this example, an investor bought a stock for $10. She received a dividend of $1 per share that was all return of capital. She will most likely not pay taxes on the $1 in the year it was received. So her cost basis falls to $9 from $10. When she sells the stock, it's trading at $20. Her capital gain is $11 instead of $10 because her cost basis was lowered by the $1 return of capital.

You can also defer your taxes based on which type of account your dividend stocks are in.

For regular dividend stocks, such as Perpetual Dividend Raisers, consider holding them in a tax-deferred account, such as an IRA, 401(k), or 529 plan. That way the dividends and reinvested dividends will grow tax-free until you retire or tap the funds for college.

Look at the difference growing the money tax-deferred makes.

Let's assume you have an IRA and you're reinvesting your dividends. The portfolio starts with a 5% yield and averages 8% dividend growth and 5% annual appreciation. After 10 years, an account that started with $100,000 will be worth about $285,000 if you reinvest the $98,500 in dividends that you received.

If those same stocks were in a taxable account where you were paying 15% taxes on those reinvested dividends every year, you'd have had to shell out almost $15,000 in taxes. To do that, either you'd have to sell some shares, which would slow down the compounding machine and lower your return to a total of $262,000, or you'd have to come up with the cash.

Of course, you'll have to pay taxes on the tax-deferred account once you tap the money in it, but you also don't necessarily have to withdraw all of the money at once, allowing the majority of the funds to continue to grow tax deferred.

Additionally, if you are no longer working, theoretically your income will be lower, so your tax rate may be as well. Remember, though, that the goal of this book is to help you generate plenty of income from your investments in retirement—enough that you'll be in the upper tax brackets if you don't have the right tax strategy.

If you're collecting income from MLPs, BDCs, REITs, or closed-end funds (with significant return of capital), you're usually better off holding those stocks in your *taxable* account.

Since the distribution is tax deferred anyway, there is no advantage to keeping it in your tax-deferred accounts. In fact, it will be a disadvantage if it replaces another income-producing investment that will be taxed as a result of being forced to reside in a taxable account because there's no room in the tax-deferred account.

If tax law does change and dividends are taxed at your ordinary income level, you should talk to your tax advisor about ways to defer taxes on those dividends. You really want those dividends to compound tax deferred over the many years. Legally protecting them from the tax man for as long as possible is going to put thousands (quite possibly tens or hundreds of thousands) more dollars in your pocket.

This chapter is just the most basic guide to taxes and dividends. Tax law has tons of variables and nuances, so once again, I urge you to talk to a tax professional if you have any questions.

Tax Law Changes

It's impossible to predict what changes to tax laws might be coming down the road. The clowns in Washington are so focused on making the opposing party look bad (something they're quite capable of on their own) that they rarely pass any decent legislation that will benefit their constituents or the nation.

But if you hear rumors of a rate hike on dividend taxes, take a look at stocks with strong insider ownership as you may be able to collect a special dividend before the rates go up.

According to Professors Michelle Hanlon at Massachusetts Institute of Technology and Jeffrey L. Hoopes at the Ohio State University, before expected tax increases, companies, especially those with large insider ownership, often pay special dividends before the higher tax rate goes into effect.[1] These special dividends may just be the next regularly scheduled quarterly dividend but pushed up a month or two.

For example, if a company pays its dividend in early February and a tax hike is coming, management may instead pay the dividend the previous December.

We saw a lot of this kind of activity in late 2010 and 2011, when the Bush tax cuts were set to expire in January 2011 and 2012. At the time, it was believed that President Obama and the Democrats would let them expire. As a result, quite a few companies paid their dividends early to take advantage of the lower tax rates.

The Bush tax cuts did get extended, so it didn't matter. All that happened was some investors got paid in December rather than January or February.

So, the next time dividend taxes are rumored to go higher, it might pay to accelerate your investments in dividend payers to capture the dividend at a lower rate.

Summary

- The current tax rate on dividends is 15%. As of this writing, it is anyone's guess whether our brilliant and practical leaders in Washington will keep the rate the same or raise it.
- You often have to pay foreign taxes on dividends of foreign companies. But you get a credit on your U.S. taxes for any foreign taxes that were paid.
- If you hold foreign stocks in an IRA or 401(k), you will not receive a foreign tax credit from the IRS.
- Consider holding your dividend stocks in a tax-deferred account, such as an IRA or 401(k).
- Do *not* hold MLPs or other investments where the majority of the distribution is a return of capital in a tax-deferred account. The distribution is already tax deferred.
- If you didn't get the message yet, talk to your tax advisor with any questions.

Note

1. Michelle Hanlon and Jeffrey L. Hoopes, "What Do Firms Do When Dividend Tax Rates Change? An Examination of Alternative Payout Responses to Dividend Tax Rate Changes," Abstract, *Journal of Financial Economics* 114, no. 1 (October 2014), www.sciencedirect.com/science/article/pii/S0304405x14001317.

Conclusion: The End of the Book, the Beginning of Your Future

Starting around the end of 2011, when it became apparent that the stock market had gone pretty much nowhere for a decade, financial advisors and writers jumped on the dividend bandwagon. Permabulls, permabears, and seemingly everyone in between suddenly started proclaiming the wisdom of investing in dividend-paying stocks as the only way to make money over the long term.

Of course, many of these people were the same ones telling you to buy Internet stocks in 2000 and 2001, just before the market tanked. In 2009, they said the world was coming to an end and you should sell everything, just before the market rallied and doubled.

Over the past three years, dividend stocks have become very popular, probably because of the publication of the first edition of this book. However, some investors were likely attracted to the stability of mature companies with long histories of returning capital back to shareholders—especially with the memories of 2008 still causing distress.

But, the main reason why dividend-paying companies have appeared on so many investors' radar screens is because of the low-interest-rate environment.

There is really nowhere else to put your money and achieve any kind of yield.

Personally, I hate that as a reason to invest in dividend payers— that there's nowhere else to go—but it's true. Banks pay nothing; money markets pay nothing. To get more than 4% on your money in a bond, you need to buy junk bonds. And most people would rather see their income increase year after year through a Perpetual Dividend Raiser than watch it stay stagnant in a bond.

Plus, with bonds being in the greatest bull market in their history, many bonds are priced above par, meaning if you hold them to maturity, you won't get all of your money back. With stocks, we know that over the long term, they go up.

I hope that in the near future, dividend stocks become less popular. While that might mean fewer book sales for me, it will mean better opportunities for dividend investors to get in at higher yields. However, as I've shown, you don't have to buy dividend stocks at the bottom to make money. Time is the more important element, not price. One can make a very valid argument that how long you invest is more important than how well you invest. Starting with the same amount, a conservative investor who underperforms the market for 30 years will have more money than one who outperforms for 20 years.

Consider this—an investor who invests $3,000 per year and earns a below market average 6% per year for 30 years will have $251,405. An investor who delays investing by 5 years will have to earn 8.4% per year to achieve the same $251,405. That 8.4% is above the historical market average. So the first investor, by investing longer, can make mistakes or have a more conservative strategy—underperforming the market—yet still wind up with the same amount as someone who beats the market.

And if the investor waits 10 years, he or she needs to generate an annual return of 12.3% per year to achieve the same results, more than double the investor's rate of return who invested for 30 years.

A 10-year difference means you need to more than double your returns. And you need to achieve a level of returns that the vast majority of professional fund managers and money managers are unable to accomplish.

Fortunately for you, you're finishing a book that taught you how to generate 12% annual returns over the long term. So even if your time horizon is shorter, you can still achieve some amazing results.

Letting your investments compound over time will enable you to reach your financial objectives.

That's what this book is all about. Although I'd love for it to become a best seller (tell your friends), my real aim is that, in 20 years, someone will tell me they read my book and they are financially secure as a result. Even better will be if they add that they taught their children the methods in this book and that those kids, now adults, are well on their way to financial independence, too.

After the first edition of *Get Rich with Dividends* came out, that's precisely what happened. I received tons of e-mail and met lots of people saying that they bought copies of the book for all of their children and grandchildren.

Hearing those stories was better than any review I've received as it meant that the strategies in this book are being passed down to younger generations and that some of those people will not go through the financial hardships that so many others did and will in the future.

Now that you have the information, it's up to you. You have no more excuses for not reaching your goals, securing your retirement, sending your kids to college. ...

You have to put some work into it—although much less than with most other investing strategies—and you have to have patience. The longer you can wait to tap into those funds, the more they will grow. And once you get past about 8 to 10 years, that money starts to really pile up each year.

In fact, I predict that unless you're in dire straits, 15 or 20 years from now, you won't want to use the money from these investments. You'll think it's smarter to find the cash somewhere else. Because the compounding dividends each year will be so substantial, you won't want to do anything that could possibly slow them down.

I truly hope this method works for you. And I implore you to teach it to your kids. By starting them young, in their thirties, twenties, or even adolescence, you'll be giving them the one of the greatest gifts you possibly can: the opportunity to be financially independent, to be able to pursue their passions, and to remove a major cause of stress from their lives.

And then they can teach the method to their children, setting up a legacy of generations that will not have anxiety about money.

Keep in mind, we're not talking about setting up generational, multimillionaire-style wealth with mansions and 12 cars and private jets. That might be possible if you invest according to the strategy in this book and the money is handed down to your children and grandchildren untouched.

But more realistically, we're talking about a strategy and discipline that, when implemented, allows you, your children, and anyone you teach it to, to live a rich life pursuing dreams and interests while not having to worry about how they'll ever be able to retire or send the kids to college or buy their first house.

How many potentially great teachers never stepped foot in a classroom because they needed to pursue better-paying jobs? How many artists never painted or composed their masterpiece for the same reason? How many men and women who love to help people did not follow their passion and become a social worker or nurse, instead toiling long hours at a job they hated just to bring home the paycheck?

I'm not naive. Life costs money. Even if you have the 10–11–12 System fully employed and working, you still need money today to pay for groceries, kids' soccer equipment, a weekend away, and the like. Simply having the system in place does not solve all of your problems.

But if you know you've got $100,000 put away that is growing at 12% per year and in 20 years it should be worth over $1 million, that does make some decisions easier. Knowing that the money is working for you, perhaps you'll feel better about going back to school for your social work degree or taking a chance at starting a new business.

Last, check out the *Get Rich with Dividends* website at www .getrichwithdividends.com. The site has helpful articles, tools, resources, and a special discount to my newsletter, the *Oxford Income Letter*, should you decide you want some assistance in choosing the very best dividend-paying stocks.

Don't forget: Look me up in 20 years, and let me know how you made out. Now go put the 10–11–12 System to work and starting getting rich with dividends.

Glossary

Activist investor   An investor who owns 5% or more of a company and demands changes from management.

American Depositary Receipt (ADR)   An instrument that trades on a U.S. exchange that represents shares (often one share) of a foreign stock.

Beta   A measure of volatility or risk. It is the correlation of a stock or portfolio's change in value in response to a move by the overall market.

Business Development Corporation (BDC)   A publicly traded private equity firm.

Call option   An option that gives the buyer the right but not the obligation to buy a security at a specific price by a certain date.

Cash flow   The amount of cash generated by a company. Often compared with earnings.

Cash flow from operations   The amount of cash generated by business activities. Does not include financing activities, such as interest payments or sale of stock.

Closed-end fund   A mutual fund that trades like a stock, based on supply and demand. Usually trades at a discount or premium to its net asset value.

Compound Annual Growth Rate (CAGR)   The average year-over-year growth rate over a period of years. It's not the simple average growth rate, but it takes into account the effect of compounding.

Compounding   The ability of an investment to earn additional money by adding previous distributions, earnings, and so on to the original amount, which generates a larger return than would be received from just the original amount.

Covered call   Selling a call, when you own the underlying stock.

Depreciation   An accounting method that lets a business expense the cost of equipment over its useful life.

Direct Stock Purchase Plan (DSPP)   A way to buy stock directly from the underlying company without going through a stockbroker.

Discount   A price less than the value of an asset.

Dividend   A cash distribution paid by a company.

Dividend Achiever   A stock that has raised its dividend for 10 or more consecutive years. List is maintained by Nasdaq OMX.

Dividend Aristocrat   A stock that is part of the Standard & Poor's (S&P) 500 and has increased its dividend for 25 or more consecutive years. List is maintained by S&P.

Dividend capture   Buying a stock just before its ex-dividend date to capture the dividend and then selling the stock shortly afterward.

Dividend Challenger   A stock that has raised its dividend for five to nine consecutive years. List is maintained by the DRiP Resource Center.

Dividend Champion   A stock that has raised its dividend for 25 or more consecutive years. Unlike a Dividend Aristocrat, a Dividend Champion is not required to be part of the S&P 500. List is maintained by the DRiP Resource Center.

Dividend Contender   A stock that has raised its dividend for 10 or more consecutive years. List is maintained by the DRiP Resource Center.

Dividend Reinvestment Program (DRIP)   A program for automatically reinvesting dividends.

Ex-dividend date   The first day that an investor can sell the stock without losing the rights to the most recently declared dividend.

Master Limited Partnership (MLP)   A publicly traded partnership. Owners are not shareholders; they are partners. MLPs have different tax considerations from stocks.

Par value   The face value of a bond or preferred stock.

Payout ratio A formula for determining the safety of the dividend. The formula is dividends paid divided by net income. You can substitute cash flow from operations or free cash flow for net income.

Perpetual Dividend Raiser A stock with a track record of raising the dividend every year.

Preferred stock Has properties of both stocks and bonds. Pays a fixed dividend, usually over a predetermined period. It is below a bond in rank as far as claims to the company's assets but above common stock.

Premium A price above the value of an asset.

Put option An option that gives the buyer the right but not the obligation to sell a security at a certain price by a specified date.

Qualified dividend Ordinary dividends that (as of 2012) are taxed at the lower 15% tax rate, rather than an investor's ordinary income tax rate.

Real Estate Investment Trust (REIT) A publicly traded partnership that invests in real estate.

Return on Equity (ROE) A measure of a company's profitability. The formula is net income divided by shareholders' equity.

Sharpe ratio A way to measure two investments' performance relative to risk.

Special dividend A one-time dividend declared by a company.

Standard deviation A measure of variability. Used in securities analysis to help determine risk.

"Y'all Must've Forgot" The worst song in the history of recorded music.

Yield The ratio of the dividend per share relative to the stock price. The formula is dividend per share divided by stock price.

About the Author

Marc Lichtenfeld is the chief income strategist of the Oxford Club and editor of the *Oxford Income Letter,* where he runs the Instant Income, Compound Income, and Retirement Catch-Up/High Yield Portfolios. Marc is also the founder and editor of *Dividend Multiplier,* the *Oxford Systems Trader,* and *Lightning Trend Trader.* Before joining the Oxford Club, he was a sell-side analyst for the contrarian Avalon Research Group and a senior columnist for TheStreet.com. Marc is regularly seen on CNBC and often appears in other national media, including WSJ.com, MarketWatch.com, and National Public Radio. A featured speaker at investment conferences, he has spoken about dividend investing at meetings all over the world. Marc is also the only published financial analyst to ring announce world championship boxing and mixed martial arts on HBO, Showtime, and ESPN.

Acknowledgments

There are many people who contributed to the publication of *Get Rich with Dividends* in one way or another.

I'd like to thank Debra Englander, formerly of John Wiley & Sons, who took my call and was instantly excited about the idea. Thank you, Debra, for making this book a reality. Also from Wiley, my editor, Tula Batanchiev, for remaining a champion for the book for several years, for motivating me to write the second edition when I didn't want to be motivated, and for all your hard work in making this book a success. This second edition would not exist without you. My editor, Judy Howarth, and my former editor, Kimberly Bernard: Thanks for all of your suggestions and improvements

Julia Guth, thank you for your support on this project and all of the others over the past eight years. Alexander Green for setting such a high standard of excellence and for your support as well. It is very much appreciated. Mike Ward for helping me get this ball rolling. Karim Rahemtulla for giving me my start at the Oxford Club and becoming a trusted mentor. Louis Basenese for guiding me through the waters during the early days, for your countless votes of confidence, and for becoming a good friend. Danielle O'Dell for everything in helping me through the process. Bill Bonner and Mark Ford for creating an incredible company that allows employees to thrive.

Matt Weinschenk for your invaluable research and contributions to this book. I couldn't have done it without you. Ryan Fitzwater for all of the excellent research. Jen Ross for creating some killer charts. Mike Kapsch for being a terrific partner on the *Oxford Income Letter* and *Wealthy Retirement*. It's a great product and I'm proud of the work we've done together. Bob Williams and Alan Gula of *Wall Street Daily* for your help and support.

All of my fellow editors at the Oxford Club: Alexander Green, Matt Carr, Steve McDonald, Sean Brodrick, Adam Sharp, and Andy Gordon. Your work helps me become a better analyst, especially when we get together to talk about the markets.

Alex Moschina for your constant efforts to turn me into a household name. I'm really glad we work so closely together, but I appreciate your friendship even more.

Laura Cadden—marketer extraordinaire. Thanks for all you do and for helping get the word out.

I am especially grateful to my friends and colleagues at the Oxford Club. It is so easy to get out of bed and come to the office every morning when I work with such intelligent, talented, and passionate people.

David Fish of the DRiP Resource Center, not only for allowing me to use your data, but also for the great work you do on behalf of dividend investors.

Alan Nadel, one of the sharpest people I know, who always immediately responded to my e-mails and was a vital sounding board. He's also been a great friend for over 30 years (how is that possible, Al?). Kevin Logan, a great trader and even better friend. I can't imagine how much less I would know about the markets if we didn't talk every day.

Eric Lichtenfeld, the best writer that I know. Thanks for always being there, giving me advice, and helping me write good. Marlowe Lichtenfeld for being an incredible sister-in-law and keeping Eric sane. Ben and Ellie Lichtenfeld for being so damn cute.

My parents, Barbara and Ed Lichtenfeld, for forcing me to stop writing "and then and then and then" in the third grade. My editor should probably thank you for that, too. Thank you for being the amazing parents that you are.

Julian and Kira. Thank you for your patience while I was writing this book. I know it stunk that I had to miss family trips and time on the weekends for a few months (again). I hope you'll think it was worth it someday.

And most of all, thank you to Holly. For everything.

Index